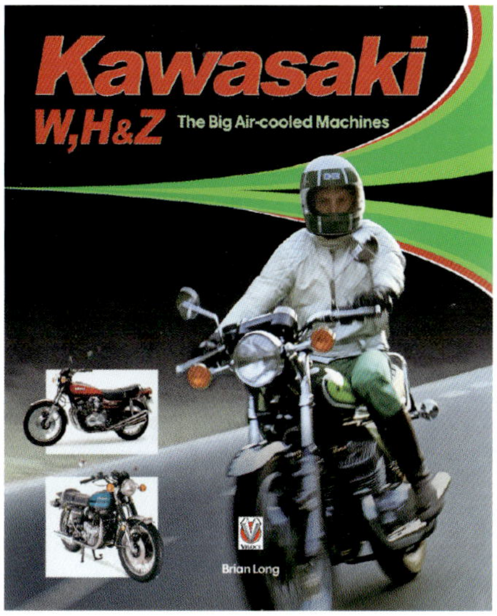
Kawasaki
W,H&Z
The Big Air-cooled Machines
Brian Long

First published in February 2019 by Veloce Publishing Limited, Veloce House, Parkway Farm Business Park, Middle Farm Way, Poundbury, Dorchester DT1 3AR, England.
Fax 01305 250479 / Tel 01305 260068 / e-mail info@veloce.co.uk / web www.veloce.co.uk or www.velocebooks.com.
ISBN: 978-1-787112-17-9 UPC: 6-36847-01217-5

British Library Cataloguing in Publication Data – A catalogue record for this book is available from the British Library. Typesetting, design and page make-up all by Veloce Publishing Ltd on Apple Mac.
Printed in India by Parksons Graphics.

TABLE OF CONTENTS

INTRODUCTION & ACKNOWLEDGEMENTS

The story of Japan's rise from the ashes after World War II is a fascinating one from so many angles. The author has covered it from the car production side, with fledgling manufacturers becoming the household names of today, the booming camera industry that knocked Germany off its pedestal, and the motorcycle trade from Suzuki's perspective. Working on this project, one can see that Suzuki and Kawasaki began their bike ventures from quite different starting points, and this is also an interesting story to tell given the influence of GHQ directives in Japan in the years immediately following the 1939-1945 conflict. Indeed, I found the story so intriguing that I have mooted the idea of a Kawasaki history book that takes in all company activities from its foundation through to the modern era – an epic tale of a rising empire and the forging of an image …

For the time being, though, having established that Kawasaki's bike odyssey was far from plain sailing in the early days (despite being able to lay claim as the oldest of the surviving 'Big Four' motorcycle manufacturers thanks to the company's links to the Meguro concern, every last ounce of Kawasaki's noteworthy 'challenge spirit' would be called upon during the early 1960s), this book concentrates on the big W1, W2 and W3 models, the speedy H1 and H2, and the legendary Z1 and Z2, with all the main markets looked at in detail on a year-by-year basis. We'll look at some of the company's other products sold alongside these at the same time, as well as the numerous racing machines that flew the flag for Kawasaki on the world stage, plus there's a section on the newer W-series models that first went into production in 1998. In the future, it's hoped we can do another volume that will take up the Z story to include the early Ninja line and its descendants, but for now, we have the chance to wallow in the nostalgia of a bygone era thanks to the efforts of a crack team based at Akashi, close to Kobe.

ACKNOWLEDGEMENTS

Most people will know me as a car guy. But my love of old bikes is very real – Barry Sheene still ranks as one of my all-time heroes, and they are deep within my blood. In fact, the only reason I haven't owned a ton of them is simply down to timing and funds. I was so into cars as a kid that I never had a penny to spare for anything else. Add in the fact that the kind of bikes I wanted required big money (and even bigger money to insure), and one can see why my enthusiasm remained largely on an academic level. As for the DNA bit, I was the first in the main family line to own a car – everyone before me had a wide range of British motorcycles for as far back as anyone can remember, and even my mother can ride a racer and help strip an engine! Her aspirations of being an engineer were soon halted by my grandfather, however, despite most of the family working on aero-engines and so on. He thought an engineer was no job for a lady, but the fact that every other old photo of her is on a different bike speaks volumes. In addition, my father was a Harley man until a bad accident made him opt for four-wheel transport, and his brother (who taught me the basics of mechanical engineering and bodywork, for which I will forever be grateful) used to race a lot in his younger days. Anyway, it's fair to say I have more than a passing interest in the subject …

I guess that DNA has surfaced of late, for I started looking for a nice classic bike to restore. This had happened many times before, but never as seriously as this, and the same thirst for knowledge that's kicked off many a car book – and even the odd camera tomb – has started me researching motorcycles in a big way. Of course, I have an unfair advantage living in Japan with a wife that can translate original material day and night, but hopefully this, not least combined with the full co-operation of the factory, will result in a volume that will satisfy even the most ardent of Kawasaki fans.

Access to the full Kawasaki archive is rare, and I'd almost given up on the idea of trying to get permission to be perfectly honest. However, Masaki Soejima – an old friend from Jaguar Japan, and a huge fan of the early Kawasakis – eventually got me in touch with the right people, with Brian Yamamoto coming forward as the saviour of the day. Our calls and meetings led to Eiko Kirino, Shigemi Tanaka and Shoji Kohama joining the fray, followed by Ryo Nishizawa and my guru Tsutomu 'Tom' Aoki to name but a few. In the end, I think we all enjoyed putting this project together, and I'm sure you will appreciate the enthusiastic input of the KTEC Heritage Program Team, as it managed to uncover a great deal of new material just for this book.

Brian Long,
Chiba City, Japan

1 KAWASAKI'S MOVE INTO BIKES

Due to the structure of the vast present-day Kawasaki empire, with the motorcycle division acting as a standalone concern, one may not be aware of the rich history attached the famous bike manufacturer, or even where the marque name comes from. It's definitely time to put that right, with a brief look at the company's foundation and activities leading up to its move into the world of motorbikes ...

Shozo Kawasaki (1837-1912). As well as lending his name to a business empire, to which he remained attached in an honorary position until his death, Kawasaki was later involved in a number of diverse activities, including politics, banking, and newspapers.

While the Kawasaki story is extremely complicated, involving a multitude of companies dealing in all manner of products, duly shuffled around on numerous occasions to suit the era (such as GHQ's destruction of the Japanese zaibatsu after WWII), the Kawasaki brand name itself is easy enough to explain, as the company's core business roots can be traced back to a small Tokyo-based shipyard originally created by Shozo Kawasaki in 1878.

Kawasaki was born in Kagoshima, on the southern island of Kyushu, on July 10, 1837. While his grandfather was a samurai, his father held the rather less glamorous position of a cloth salesman, as the golden age of the samurai had already come to an end. As this era finished, though, another was beginning, with the Meiji Restoration opening Japan's doors to outside trade on a far larger scale than ever before. Nagasaki, to the north of Kagoshima but still on Kyushu, officially became a free port in 1859. Kawasaki had moved there at 17 following the death of his father, dealing with the Dutch traders to make enough money to survive, whilst learning foreign languages in the evening.

Kawasaki eventually moved to Osaka on the main island of Honshu in 1863, opening a marine shipping

LEFT The Kawasaki trademark, with a highly stylised version of the kanji for kawa, or river in English. Often mounted on a maritime flag, the symbol has been seen in various forms over the years, even making an appearance on the early motorcycle tank badges, and has recently been revived to celebrate the 120th anniversary of the company.

BELOW The 727-ton *Iyomaru* being launched from the Kawasaki Dockyard in Kobe in 1897. Kawasaki's first ship was the 80-ton wooden-hulled *Hokkaimaru* of 1878.

business, but life was still hard at this time, with the entrepreneur experiencing a number of shipwrecks along the way, and ultimately having to declare bankruptcy. By the end of the decade, he'd joined a sugar company in what is today's Okinawa – a chain of islands far to the south of Kyushu – and was duly asked by the Ministry of Finance to investigate shipping routes to the Japanese mainland. This is where Kawasaki's luck changed, for his work for the Ministry led to him gaining an executive position within the Japan Mail Steamboat Shipping Company – a business created at the suggestion of Kawasaki.

During this time, Kawasaki's trust in western ships increased to the point where he suggested making these faster, more stable iron-hulled boats domestically, and with the support of a proud fellow Satsuma province man, Masayoshi Matsukata of the Finance Ministry, the Kawasaki Tsukiji Shipyard was duly established on land rented from the government in April 1878. Operations were expanded in 1881 via another yard in Kobe, Hyogo Prefecture (to the west of Tokyo), as the superior shipping routes and potential for growth held far greater appeal than the Tokyo site. Eventually, the businesses were merged to become the Kawasaki Dockyard in May 1886, with Kobe becoming the spiritual home of Kawasaki thereafter.

MATSUKATA'S INFLUENCE

While the first section establishes the roots of the brand name and the company's early links with the coastal city of Kobe, it has to be said that Kawasaki's growth as an engineering giant at the start of the 20th century can be attributed to a gentleman by the name of Kojiro Matsukata, rather than Shozo Kawasaki.

Booming on the back of repair orders generated by the first Sino-Japanese War, the shipyard was eventually incorporated as the Kawasaki Dockyard Co Ltd on October 15, 1896, with Kojiro Matsukata named as the first President of the firm. Already advancing in age and with no living sons old enough (only a daughter), Matsukata (the third son of Masayoshi Matsukata, Kawasaki's backer, who'd actually served as Japan's Prime Minister by this time) was seen as the ideal person to continue Kawasaki's work and vision, and history would duly prove him to be a good choice. Indeed, he would continue as President until 1928.

It would be nice to spend more time covering the Matsukata years, for they were full of interesting stories, but unfortunately the scope of this book will only allow us a brief overview of the company's activities – enough to explain how certain branches came about, and how they ultimately fit in with today's sprawling business empire.

Naturally, the firm was mainly concerned with shipbuilding in the early days, constructing around eight ships a year, with iron gradually giving way to steel hulls in the mid-1890s. Orders for bigger ships were accepted after a huge dry dock was opened next to the old yard in Kobe in 1902, leading to the first of many commissions from the Imperial Japanese Navy – for submarines (based on modified John P Holland designs from America), as well as warships, marking a new era of domestically-produced naval

RIGHT It was a natural progression for Kawasaki to move into automotive chassis production and coachbuilding, with the firm concentrating on trucks and buses in the main, like this bus based on a Mitsubishi chassis, delivered to Japan's Ministry of Railways in 1934. Notwithstanding, there were also some exceptional passenger cars, with Art Deco catalogues boasting of these 'pure Japanese' automobiles. However, the need for military aeroplane production was more pressing, and majority of this side of the business was passed to Automobile Industries (now Isuzu) in the late-1930s.

BELOW The first batch of Kawasaki steam locomotives, built in 1911. These 4-4-0 locos, Japan's first domestically produced model as it happens, required a coal tender. Many SL variants would follow in due course, while one of the other giants in the game, the Kisha Seizo concern, duly merged with KHI in 1972.

vessels. The marine transportation side of the business was eventually hived off in 1919 to become the eminent K Line concern.

In the meantime, like many of Japan's warships from the turn of the century, most of its early trains were imported from Britain. As it happens, Kawasaki had been thinking of building locomotives and rolling stock for quite some time, allowing the company to ride out the harsh peaks and troughs associated with the boat business, but development plans were hampered by the war with Russia. At last, in May 1907, a new factory was opened close to the shipyards, more inland and a mile or so to the southwest of them, with an order book already full thanks to a shift in government policy on the purchase of railway hardware. The factory (today's Hyogo Works) began producing freight wagons and passenger carriages straight away, before building the first of many steam locomotives in 1911, and would duly make things like castings and metal bridge girders as well. The timing was right, for financial woes both domestically and abroad led to a drastic cut in the workforce – a cut that, had Kawasaki been relying purely on shipbuilding, would have surely meant a swift end for the business.

Meanwhile, a tie-up with GEC of America led to the company gaining electric motors for trains, while steam turbines for marine applications were being produced at the original Kawasaki site, now known as the Kobe Works; there were also several flirtations with diesel engines via European firms.

The Imperial Japanese Navy had been using aeroplanes since 1912, with the army adopting aircraft at around the same time, as well as airships. Many of the early machines were sourced from French makers, although by the middle of the Great War, thanks to a bill passed by the government, Japan was already set on a course of creating its own aeroplanes, even though the results would be some time coming. The main players were the Nakajima concern, north of Tokyo, the Mitsubishi Shipyard in Kobe, and, from July 1918, Kawasaki, with the Kobe works (right next to Mitsubishi, as it happens) acting as the base for aircraft activities. The first Kawasaki Otsu Type I prototypes, using Salmson technology from France, were completed at the end of 1922. No less than 300 were built by 1927, but by this time, despite greater involvement in steel production etc, due to a downturn in the economy, Kawasaki was in dire straits.

Kojiro Matsukata donated a great deal of his personal fortune to keep the company afloat, but still felt the ultimate responsibility lay at his feet, and he duly resigned in 1928 – the year in which the rolling stock business at the Hyogo Works was separated to become an independent firm. For the record, the Kawasaki Rolling Stock Manufacturing Co Ltd built a large number of trucks and buses from 1929 to 1942, and even created the odd luxury automobile along the way using the Rokko and Rokkogo brand names.

For the record, Matsukata died in June 1950, but he could rest easy in the knowledge that he'd laid many of the important foundation stones that allowed Kawasaki to become a formidable giant in the world of engineering.

BELOW The Akashi works as we know them today, under construction on land bought in 1938, with the engine test block in the background. The building can still be seen at the Akashi site to this day.

THE BIRTH OF KHI

The aeroplane business was spun off to become the Kawasaki Aircraft Co Ltd in 1937. By this time, it had moved on from the Otsu Type I via Dornier technology, leading to the creation of a new and highly-successful line of all-metal military machines, as well as a new airframe facility in Gifu, close to Nagoya. With war clouds looming, in China and the world stage, the aircraft manufacturing side would become increasingly important for Japan, with activities accelerating at a staggering pace, as is often the case in times

BELOW Kawasaki Ki-48 light bomber fitted with a prototype Ne-0 jet engine (Japan's first) for testing purposes. This rare picture, courtesy of the KHI Hayashi Collection, was taken at Gifu in late December 1943.

BOTTOM The Akashi factory photographed after a January 1945 bombing raid by US B-29s, in which a third of the plant was destroyed. It suffered a much heavier attack six months later, but aeroplane production had already left the Akashi works by then, such was the damage caused by earlier raids; the fact that Kawasaki was responsible for building almost one-fifth of Japan's air force in WWII made it a legitimate target. One can just make out a handful of tiny aeroplanes to the left of the factory.

BELOW The Gifu works in the spring of 1944, full of Ki-61 'Hien' fighters. Designed by Takeo Doi, it was powered by a Daimler-Benz water-cooled engine built under licence as the Ha-40 (or Ha-140 in its modified, more powerful form) at Kawasaki's Akashi facility. In addition, Kawasaki made a huge number of radial powerplants, and was also at the forefront of Japanese jet engine technology, while more airframes were produced in Miyazaki, further south. There was even a factory built in Singapore, but Japan surrendered before it became fully operational.

of conflict. The same was true for the shipbuilding side, too, of course. But an interesting development was the purchase of more land in Nishi-Akashi, just a few miles to the west of Kobe, in 1938. This would be a shadow factory for building aircraft (both airframes and aero-engines), and once officially completed in September 1940, would play a very important role in the Kawasaki story, particularly with regard to the company's motorcycles – the core subject of this book ...

In the meantime, in December 1939, the mainstream line of the business changed its name from Kawasaki Dockyard Co Ltd to a more suitable Kawasaki Heavy Industries Ltd (or KHI), as this covered a far greater range of activities than the original moniker implied. By this time, of course, the world found itself plunged into another global conflict ...

THE EARLY POSTWAR YEARS

First there was the invasion of Manchuria, and the creation of a puppet state, followed by the Second Sino-Japanese War

RIGHT The Banshu gear factory, which was a major contributor in helping Kawasaki bounce back after the war.

BELOW RIGHT The KAL-1 light transport aircraft of 1953, powered by a 260bhp Lycoming engine. Kawasaki had actually built its own version of the air-cooled flat-six, called the KAE-240, but it was never used in the end. Other planes and helicopters, as well as numerous types of aero-engines, revived the aircraft side of the business.

that kicked off in 1937 and continued until Japan officially became involved in WWII, siding with the Axis Powers after being snubbed in the aftermath of the Great War of 1914-1918. The country had therefore been fighting abroad to some degree for most of the 1930s and the first half of the 1940s, and the requirements of the government served Kawasaki well (perhaps too well at times due to a distinct shortage of space and manpower), from obvious things like aircraft and ships for military use, through to trains for a new rail network to be built in Manchuria. However, this naturally made the various Kawasaki sites a prime target, with relentless bombing raids carried out by the Americans before Emperor Hirohito announced Japan's surrender over the radio on August 15, 1945.

One cannot really appreciate the state Japan was left in after VJ Day without seeing contemporary pictures – the Americans had used tons of incendiary devices during their air raids, wiping out huge swathes of wooden housing, while regular bombs saw to what was left, knocking out sturdier structures and roads. Tokyo, Nagoya and Osaka were in ruins, with over 8,000,000 homeless on the streets, food was in short supply, and the trains left running were packed with folks trying to trade their last belongings, as their cash was basically worthless due to escalating inflation. Transport was desperately needed to get the country mobile again, but it had to be cheap to buy, frugal and tough.

Such was the devastation, followed by a tight grip on material supply and usage imposed by GHQ (as well as wider restrictions on what firms, especially the larger zaibatsu like Kawasaki, were able to build, scuttling any chances of Japan rearming) that lasted until the Allied forces (led by General Douglas MacArthur for most of the occupation, with General Matthew Ridgway eventually taking his place) finally pulled out of Tokyo in 1952, that even though there was a definite requirement for motor vehicles, few were in a position to fill the gap in the market.

In the eyes of MacArthur, with so many left with nothing after the conflict, exports were always going to be the key to post-war recovery, so the production of smaller, high-value items like cameras was encouraged, bringing much-needed foreign currency into the country. This seemed like a reasonable idea, and indeed, one only needs to look at the success of companies like Nikon and Canon to see there was mileage in it, but, somewhat ironically, it was US military orders for the Korean War effort that got the auto makers rolling again – another war helping to repair the damage from an earlier one.

Meanwhile, Kawasaki was given an order for a new batch of steam trains in 1946; electric trains were also produced, but the aircraft and marine side of the business was basically crippled at this time, leading to dramatic cuts in the workforce and the closure of seven satellite factories to leave just two in one particular county, although restrictions on ships and steam turbines were gradually eased during 1948, and a huge order from Norway for a brand new tanker revived hopes in the shipyard after building nothing but fishing boats for a while. Ultimately, by 1956, with Kawasaki's help, Japan had overtaken Britain as the world's number one shipbuilder. However, the need to survive in the meantime saw the company making things like vehicle bodies, small three-wheeled trucks (in conjunction with Mitsubishi and Toyo Kogyo, later known as Mazda), specialist gear wheels, automotive radiators, conveyor systems, machines for producing chemical fibres, welding equipment, fire extinguishers, and even cooking utensils and typewriters later on.

Having restarted operations at the end of 1946 (with healthy worldwide exports beginning in 1949), the steelmaking division was eventually hived off to become the Kawasaki Steel Corporation in 1950, and at around the same time a number of other arms of the business were renamed and separated, although they would all come back under the KHI umbrella in due course in more familiar forms and sporting another new set of monikers to signify a return to normality. Bell 47D helicopters were eventually built under licence at Akashi soon after Japan's ban on producing aeronautical machines was lifted in 1952, and transport planes were duly constructed at the Gifu works, too. Then came an interesting development that would ultimately shape the future of the Kawasaki company, giving birth to a motorcycle business that would become the face of Kawasaki in the eyes of most people ...

A TWO-WHEELER FORAY

A handful of motorcycle manufacturers, such as Meguro, Showa, Rikuo and Miyata (who had all been furnished with military contracts for their bikes, incidentally), had gingerly gone back to what they knew best following the end of the war, while the Nakajima Aircraft Co (later Fuji Heavy Industries, the owners of the Subaru brand) and Mitsubishi started making scooters. At the other end of the scale, Soichiro Honda decided to use some war surplus two-stroke 50cc generator engines to power bicycles as a cheap form of transport. While the Kawasaki aeroplane business was slowly coming back to life, a decision was made to follow the likes of Honda (and ultimately Suzuki, for that matter, with its successful Power Free being launched in June 1952) in producing motorized bicycles.

Planning had actually started not that long after the war, with Takatsuki being earmarked for four-stroke motorcycle engine production, while the Banshu plant, with only light wartime damage, would make two-stroke units to power bicycles.

The main Akashi works was still in a very sorry state at this time, with GHQ forbidding repairs on factories related to war production, but something had to be done, and Kawasaki Kikai Kogyo (the Kawasaki Machine Industry Co Ltd) was formed on May 1, 1950 as a successor of the Kawasaki Sangyo concern, itself an evolution of Kawasaki

LEFT The KE-1 engine, with twin exhaust pipes. The KE-2 was a direct development of this unit, while the KE-3, used by Amano and built alongside the KE-2, had a single exhaust outlet.

BELOW An early KB-1 two-stroke unit mounted on a Dainippon Kikai Kogyo frame to make the sturdy Denko machine. Later models carried Meihatsu badging on both the fuel tank and the engine, usually written 'Meihatu' in accordance with the era. It's actually the same thing, just a different style of translation.

Aircraft following the end of the war, with bases at Akashi, the Banshu Takinocho gear-making factory a few miles north of Akashi, the Takatsuki works, north of Osaka, and, for a while at least, a Kobe site that was actually closed in July that year.

Development started on a 148cc (57mm x 58mm) air-cooled ohv single at Takatsuki around 1949, capable of delivering around 4bhp at 4500rpm. With a separate transmission, the first KE-1 prototypes (with KE standing for Kawasaki Engine) were running in 1950, although suitable outlets were not forthcoming until the Dainippon Kikai Kogyo concern of Tokyo decided to adopt the unit for its Hikari L-type model in 1952. Full-scale production of the four-stroke KE-1 began in February 1953, with 160 made before a pair of modified KE-2 and KE-3 engines were introduced five months later. No less than 1600 KE-2 power-units and 650 KE-3s were built between July 1953 and the spring of 1954, with Amano also taking engines by this time for its RSY model.

Having received advice from Tokyo University's Kiyoshi Tomizuka (the man that had led the famed Koken-Ki long-distance aircraft project), the two-stroke project kicked off in 1951, but the end result – the KB-1 – came to market sooner than the four-stroke unit, in January 1953. This 58cc (42mm x 42mm) air-cooled single-cylinder lump gave 1.6bhp at 4500rpm, and around 1500 were supplied to Dainippon Kikai Kogyo for its Denko machine by the spring of 1954. This was also modified to become the slightly more powerful 2.1bhp KB-2 with an integrated transmission and central frame mounting (2800 made between August 1953 and July 1954), while the KB-3 was only built for a few months in the middle of 1954, although no less than 1860 of these 2.5bhp units were produced during this time, with Okamoto having also joined the client list. By the way, the 58cc KB-series engines were built at the Akashi Chaenba site rather than the Banshu works from March 1953, bringing Akashi into the picture earlier than expected.

In the meantime, like so many of its contemporaries, Dainippon Kikai Kogyo found itself in financial trouble, and, as its main customer, this was a huge loss for the fledgling

BELOW The Meihatsu 'Fukyu-go' of December 1953, seen here with the KB-1 engine. It could also be fitted with the centrally-mounted KB-2, making the machine look more like a proper motorcycle.

BELOW A production version of the Kawasaki scooter of 1954 vintage, employing the 2.1bhp KB-2 two-stroke engine with an integrated transmission. This 90,000 yen machine, the first bike to bear the Kawasaki badge, was made at the Gifu plant, but only about 200 were made before sales came to an end. Earlier plans submitted in 1947 for a four-stroke 750cc Kawasaki three-wheeler had been ditched almost immediately.

Kawasaki motorcycle engine business. To save the situation, Kawasaki brought in eight workers from Dainippon and formed a sales arm using the Meihatsu Kogyo moniker (Meihatsu being an abbreviation of the various kanji for Kawasaki Kikai Akashi Kojo Sei Hatsudoki, incidentally) on December 15, 1953, taking over the Dainippon operation in Tokyo at same time. As such, any machines built thereafter carried the Meihatsu name, although the home market was an increasingly difficult arena in which to survive (especially after Honda introduced the amazingly successful Cub), so, if one is to be perfectly frank, the idea was poorly rewarded for many years.

However, following the merger of Kawasaki Aircraft Kogyo and Kawasaki Kikai Kogyo in February 1954 (keeping the former name only in the reshuffle), plus a separate merger of the Banshu, Takatsuki and Chaenba bike operations, Kawasaki-Meihatsu Kogyo KK was duly formed as a new subsidiary in the summer, signifying the intention to start producing complete motorcycles, gradually syphoning Meihatsu production away from the antiquated Dainippon factory in Katsushika-ku, Tokyo. While the Gifu plant continued much the same as before, the other old factories were brought together and moved to the confusingly named Kobe works over 1954 and 1955, headed by Fukuzo Yamamoto. For the record, the Kobe plant name is confusing because it was situated in Nishi-Akashi (Western Akashi) rather than Kobe – something brought about by the Mayor of the time proposing that Akashi would become part of Kobe City, although the move was never carried through, and the Akashi moniker was finally applied to the site in 1969.

Before that, though, by April 1954, there was also a four-stroke 247cc (68mm x 68mm) KH-1 air-cooled ohv single-cylinder engine being marketed. Based on German technology and rated at 11.7bhp at 5700rpm, 1386 KH-1 units had been made at the Akashi factory by the end of 1956, with users including the likes of Amano, Rocket and Ito (makers of the IMC). Lacking a decent sales route and with the marketplace still flooded with domestic makers at the time, turnkey four-stroke machines were still not considered part of the plan, and in the end, with falling demand as manufacturers fell by wayside (often incurring bad debts), the company decided to stop supplying four-stroke engines to outside concerns.

Notwithstanding, two-stroke engine development continued, with the 76cc (48mm x 42mm) KB-83 3.3bhp air-cooled single being introduced for the later version of

BELOW LEFT The 1955 IMC M-type, powered by the KH-1 four-stroke engine. While the KH-1 was designed by Tetsuro Takahashi at the Takatsuki factory (Takahashi later moved to the jet engine side of the business) in early 1953, all KH engines were built at the Akashi plant.

BELOW RIGHT The Meihatsu 125 Super of spring 1957, powered by the 6bhp KB-5A unit. Later in the year, the Super and Deluxe grades were merged to become one model, built alongside the 125-500 and 125-600, which continued with the strict KB-5 engine.

MAIN PICTURE The 125,000 yen Meihatsu 125-500, with a KB-5 engine (note the 'Kawasaki' name on the engine case) and plunger-type rear suspension. The 125-600, launched at the same time and 10,000 yen cheaper, had a rigid back-end, which looked attractive, but was hardly suited to the rough Japanese roads of the time. At least the 125 Deluxe, introduced in February 1956, along with the sportier 125 Super that followed a couple of months later, came with a modern swing-arm rear suspension.

the Meihatsu 60-II and the 80-III models in October 1954, and the 123cc (53mm x 56mm) KB-5 unit four months later. Rated at 5.5bhp, the KB-5 had its single cylinder leaning forwards to allow for a neater installation, and came with an integral three-speed transmission operated by the left foot. It duly found service in the Meihatsu 125-500 (or 125-V) and 125-600 (aka the 125-VI, introduced alongside the 125-V in July 1955 as the company's first proper motorcycles), plus the 125 Super and 125 Deluxe bikes, with 6000 built by the end of 1956, and was the basis for Kawasaki's two-stroke engines that followed for a decade.

With Kawasaki Aircraft having injected a reasonable amount of money into the Kawasaki-Meihatsu Kogyo KK operation in early 1956, by 1957, all of the company's four-stroke technology had been brought together and refined within a new engine department, with some interesting results, for the bike world was an increasingly difficult arena in which to survive (indeed, Japan's motorcycle makers had dwindled from over 200 in 1953 to half that amount in 1957, with the number set to fall off rapidly thereafter), especially for machines like the two-stroke Meihatsu, with limited sales and service outlets due to a lack of full-blooded commitment, whilst having to face up to the might of Honda and a moped boom brought about by domestic rule changes issued in 1958. Fortunately, despite heavy losses year after year, the Kawasaki group had the funds at its disposal to keep things going even when perhaps the most sensible thing would have been to throw the towel in long before ...

Variations on a theme

Given the core subject of this book, it's worth outlining the differences between a traditional Otto-cycle petrol engine and its two-stroke counterpart. We may as well go into the advantages and negative aspects of both units too, as they are quite different in terms of character and efficiency.

The Otto-cycle is a term for the four-stroke system applied to internal combustion engines. The word 'Otto' comes out of respect for Nikolaus August Otto (father of the four-stroke principle), while the four-stroke moniker itself describes the four piston movements necessary to complete one combustion cycle in conjunction with suitable inlet and exhaust valve operation, a method of igniting a measured fuel/air mixture, and a crankshaft with offset crankpins to keep pistons moving in the desired direction. The four 'strokes' can be summed up as follows:

Intake – As the piston moves down the cylinder, a suitable fuel/air mixture is drawn into the combustion chamber through the open inlet valve. The exhaust valve is closed at this stage.

Compression – Both valves are closed, allowing the fuel/air mixture to be compressed within the combustion chamber as the piston rises in the cylinder.

Power – With both valves closed, the fuel/air mixture is ignited either by a spark or an increase in heat through extreme pressure (via a higher compression ratio, as in the diesel engine), the resulting controlled explosion pushing the piston back down again.

Exhaust – As the piston starts to rise again, the inlet valve remains shut, but the exhaust valve opens allowing burnt gases to exit the combustion chamber.

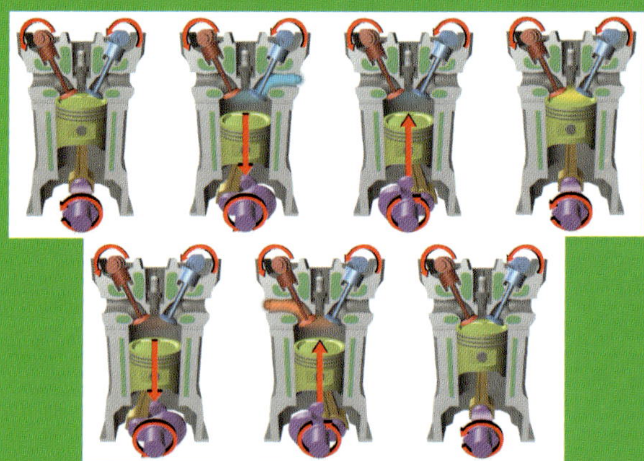

Illustrations courtesy of Wapcaplet/Creative Commons.

With hybrid vehicles now commonplace on today's roads, one may hear about Atkinson- or Miller-cycle engines, but the basic theory is the same as the Otto-cycle. With a two-stroke ICE, one follows the same sequence but in two piston strokes instead of four, by taking away the traditional valve system and using the piston's shape and travel combined with careful port positioning to complete the combustion cycle.

This allows these units to be lighter and more compact, as well as less complicated, meaning they are cheaper and easier to manufacture – these benefits are further increased with air cooling. They also deliver a power stroke on every rotation of the crankshaft (instead of every second rotation, as on a four-stroke engine), giving them a high power-to-weight ratio, faster acceleration and a free-revving character.

As it happens, the two-stroke idea has been around for a long time, since 1889 in fact, with the Englishman Joseph Day being responsible for the two-stroke as we know it. His designs were quickly refined, with the classic 'crankcase-scavenged' two-stroke unit coming about after a modification by Frederick Cock, who worked for Day's engineering company. This is how the engine works:

Upstroke – As the piston moves to the top of the cylinder, it compresses the air/fuel/oil mixture already delivered via the transfer port, and exposes the intake port beneath it as soon as it reaches TDC (top dead centre) in the case of a cylinder wall port (a reed valve or rotary disc valve could also be employed for intake purposes, as seen in the illustrations, with slightly quicker induction timing). This allows a fresh charge to be drawn into the crankcase. The exhaust port is blocked off by the piston skirt, as is the transfer port that connects the combustion chamber and the crankcase. Compression is followed by combustion, with a spark igniting the mixture to push the piston back down again.

Downstroke – As the piston moves downwards, this closes the intake and exposes the exhaust port, with the underside of the piston starting to pre-compress the fresh charge. On reaching BDC (bottom dead centre), the transfer port is now fully exposed, allowing the partially compressed charge to move from the crankcase into the combustion chamber and push out any remaining exhaust gases. The weight of the flywheel sees to it that the piston starts moving upwards again, first covering all ports and compressing the mixture before the intake port is exposed (or opened in the case of a reed valve or rotary disc valve) for the cycle to start again.

The two-stroke power-unit can boast a number of worthwhile advantages. However, while oil passages are not required (saving a fortune on machining), a small amount of engine lubricant has to be mixed with the fuel, meaning extremely high levels of particulate matter (PM) emissions

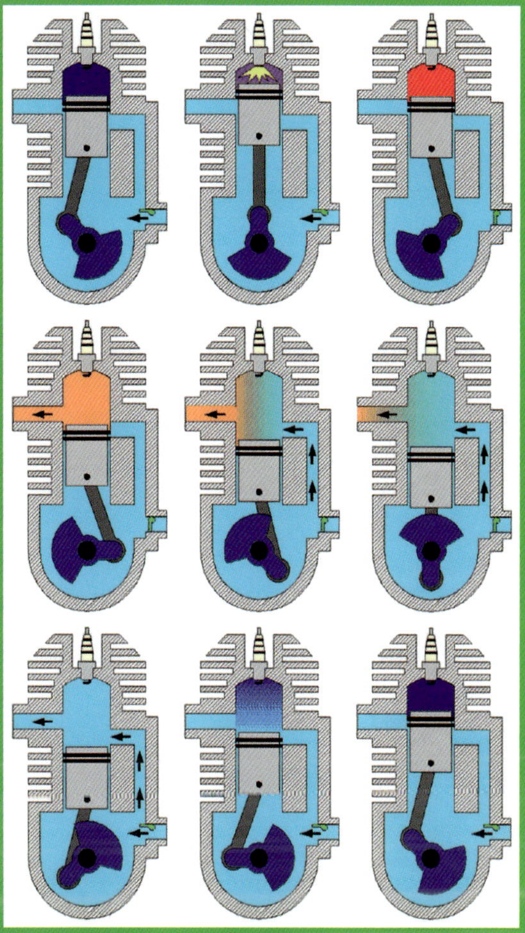

Illustrations courtesy of A Schierwagen using OpenOffice Draw/Creative Commons.

from cross-contamination; due to the layout of the combustion chamber this more often than not leads to part of the air-fuel charge being wasted, leaking through the exhaust port before it is ignited. While thoughtful exhaust pipe designs can reduce this inevitable waste to a minimum, HC emissions are therefore very bad as a result, although CO and NOx emissions are actually lower than those of four-stroke engines, generally speaking.

There were a few automobile manufacturers that used two-stroke engines, with Saab being one of the last notables – ultimately, while they tend to release more power for a given displacement compared to an Otto-cycle unit, the lack of low-end torque and a fairly narrow power band makes the two-stroke option less attractive in a heavy application like a car. But as fuel consumption concerns increased and the environmental damage became more apparent, even motorcycle makers started moving almost exclusively toward four-stroke units at the end of the 1970s.

RIGHT The Akashi works (or 'Kobe Manufacturing' works officially) as they looked in 1958. Another huge building had been added in the foreground by the following year.

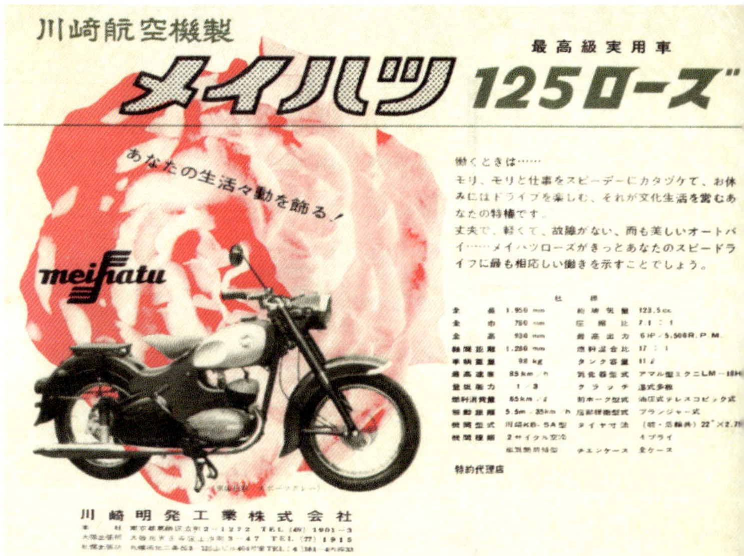

BELOW RIGHT Brochure from the author's collection showing the 1958 Meihatsu Rose.

ANY OTHER BUSINESS

In the background, from the tail-end of 1955, the Akashi factory was engaged in developing a new line of KF two-stroke engines for agricultural machinery, and was also working on diesel truck engines, ultimately leading to yet another expansion of the Akashi site in 1958, as well as an interesting tie-up with Porsche of Germany. Other business spheres included a move into electric power generation via Kawasaki Denki Seizo in 1959 (a company that duly merged with Fuji Denki in 1968), and links with the nuclear industry were forged during the same era.

In the meantime, the Meihatsu brand, which could quite easily be considered the starting point of today's Kawasaki Motors, was still being nurtured. In April 1957, the KB-5 was refined to become the more powerful KB-5A, with 6bhp and improved low-speed torque delivery. The nearside case had a new 'Kawasaki' logo with stronger graphics, while the offside one featured the Kawasaki flag. It was used on the new 125 Deluxe and Super models initially, which gained pressed steel frames at this time. There was also an FA-1 125cc prototype bike completed in August 1957, powered by a KB-6 engine, although it was sadly never produced. The Ace did make it to the showrooms, however, being a fresh Super model in reality, and introduced in February 1958; the new Super was in effect the old Deluxe. In addition, the Rose was released in August 1958, featuring the KB-5A unit in a new frame.

Meanwhile, the summer of 1958 brought with it the KB-25 engine, which was basically a twin-cylinder version of the KB-5A. Sporting the same bore and stroke measurements but twice the number of pots, the displacement went up to 247cc, which released 16bhp at 6000rpm. Hooked up to an advanced four-speed transmission, the KB-25 was fitted to the Meihatsu Crown, which made its debut at the Tokyo Show in October 1958, displayed alongside the 1959 MY versions of the Super, Ace and Rose models.

Spring 1959 witnessed the launch of the 123cc KB-5AS engine, which was basically a 6bhp KB-5A unit equipped with an electric starter. Both the Meihatsu Ace and the late Super were fitted with this single, although it was modified in September to become the shortlived 8bhp KB-6AS that was used in the latest version of the 125-60 that was launched that month. There was also a KB-7AS variant, but it was never put into production, as time was running out for the KB powerplant line. At the end of the day, huge losses had led to the parent company and Daiichi Bank calling for an end to the two-stroke motorcycle engine business, which was accounting for only 15 per cent of the income from Kawasaki's motor-building exploits.

There were a number of reasons for the company's lack of success. One, it had entered the arena too late to take full

BELOW The attractive Meihatsu Crown, fitted with a two-stroke twin-cylinder engine. Unfortunately, despite there being a standard and sports variant, it was not a commercial success, but it does feature a simple 'M' tank badge (duly adopted on other 'new generation' models from late-1959 onwards), clearing up the 'Meihatsu' or 'Meihatu' question once and for all – at least until one looked at a catalogue ...

BOTTOM The KB-5AS engine seen on its own (inset), and in situ in the 125 Ace 59, launched in April 1959. The 'S' suffix denoted an electric self-starter system.

advantage of it, and with bikes made in small volumes, there was little chance of making a profit with competitive prices applied. Two, the sales and service network was nowhere near strong enough to attract and – just as importantly – keep customers. With gas turbine work requiring a huge amount of time and money to get it off the ground, to bridge the gap, on Christmas Day 1959, it was decided once and for all that a new approach would be adopted for the motorbike arm, with complete machines to be made using the Kawasaki nameplate, and with the full backing of Kawasaki Aircraft (or KAC) instead of merely a passing interest.

For a change, there was some good timing here, for Japan had just become the world's number one motorcycle manufacturer in terms of production volume, prompting Honda, Suzuki and Yamaha to hold a meeting at Hamamatsu on export strategy in order to keep up momentum, and the Japanese government was keener than usual to promote industry, announcing a plan in late 1960 that was hoped would double the country's GDP through engineering and other industrial spheres.

By September 1960, part of a brand new 8000 square metre production facility was completed and ready for action at the sprawling Akashi works; the factory (internally identified by the number 24) was fully-operational two months later. As such, a new chapter in Kawasaki's history had begun, although the marque still had some tough lessons to learn.

In the meantime, the Meihatsu 125 New Ace and 125 Sports had been launched in the summer of 1960 (both powered by the KB-6AS), alongside the 247cc Crown 60, which now came with an electric starter instead of a kickstart only. The Sports model, though, would remain a prototype that did the show scene, and in September 1960, Meihatsu's motorcycle production rights were passed to Kawasaki Aircraft. Within three months, only a sales office belonging to Meihatsu remained in Tokyo, as everything else was brought together at the Akashi works. In May 1961, the Meihatsu firm was renamed Kawasaki Jidosha Sales Ltd, which, after a few more name changes, eventually became Kawasaki Motors Corporation in 1993.

BELOW The Kawasaki stand at an Osaka trade fair, with the Crown and 'new generation' 125-60 on display, as well as a selection of KF engines for farming applications, a model of a train, and a picture of the P2V-7 aircraft, the first one being completed by the company in September 1959.

BOTTOM A fine array of Meihatsu machines employed by Kansai Denryoku, an electrical generating firm based in Osaka.

BELOW Kawasaki opened a small test course at Akashi on October 4, 1960. The tape was cut by Fukuzo Yamamoto (left), who was in overall charge of the Akashi (or Kobe Manufacturing) site, as well as the head of the motorcycle department by this time. Indeed, Yamamoto was one of the key figures behind Kawasaki making a positive move into the bike world, albeit as a stopgap to allow aeronautical development to continue initially.

The Meguro Marque

Having gained experience of engines with an iron-working firm, the Meguro Manufacturing Co was established by Nobuji Murata close to Meguro Fudo (or Ryusen Temple) in Tokyo in 1924. Murata was duly joined by an ex-naval man, Takaji Suzuki, and, while there was a brief flirtation with the Giant motorbike (a Harley impersonator financed by Count Kuwashi Katsu), Meguro quickly became known for being a specialist in the field of engines and transmissions for motorcycles and three-wheelers.

It wasn't until 1937 that firm built its first complete motorbike – the Meguro Z97. This was powered by a four-stroke 498cc ohv single rated at 11bhp, hooked up to a three-speed transmission operated by hand, and was successful enough to prompt the management into making Meguro into a limited company in February 1939.

Production was naturally turned over to the war effort once WWII got underway, but bikes were revived after the conflict in 1948, with a new version of the big 498cc single sold alongside a pair of smaller 143cc and 248cc four-stroke singles from 1950. The range was duly refined year after year, with entry-level models coming and going, but the 498cc Z remained Meguro's signature product, sold in Z7 guise from 1956 to the middle of 1961. By that time, Meguro had introduced an even larger 651cc twin in the form of the Senior T1 of May 1955 vintage, which was updated and made until 1960.

After modernizing its range in the summer of 1958, some would say too late, Meguro became a publicly listed company in the following year. During 1960, in addition to the old favourites built to order, Meguro listed the 123cc CA and CAS models, the 164cc Ranger DA with a sohc unit, the 247cc Junior S7, and the attractive 496cc Stamina K1, which was basically a 295,000 yen combination of the old Z7 and T2 grades, using the British BSA for reference (in fact, many of the Meguros can trace their roots – or at the very least, their inspiration – back to European machines). On November 30 that year, though, Meguro signed a deal with Kawasaki that would see Kawasaki taking on the tiddlers, and Meguro only making bikes with engines displacing 250cc or more. This move, whilst giving the Tokyo concern access to smaller machines and Kawasaki an established dealer network, thus helping both parties, basically signalled the beginning of the end for Meguro. Many saw this happening at the Meguro works, as it happens, sparking lengthy strikes and industrial unrest ...

Meanwhile, the 50cc (41mm x 38mm) MA and MAS models were brought out in 1961, being the first and only two-strokes sold using the Meguro nameplate. They were not a commercial success, though, and the few bikes that followed were more traditional – four-stroke twins and singles with engine capacities ranging from 496cc at one extreme to 248cc at the other.

Meguro and Kawasaki Jidosha Sales Ltd were brought together in August 1961 to handle sales, although Meguro was already struggling financially, being forced to move its factory to Yokohama at the end of the year (cutting its workforce from 700 to just 165 at the same time), and Kawasaki-Meguro Manufacturing was duly formed in October 1962; four months later, the outfit was swallowed wholesale by Kawasaki Aircraft, with most of the key Meguro staff being left in the cold. The final strict Meguro model – as opposed to a double-named machine, like the SGT – the 288cc Argus J8, was launched in May 1963, with the marque ultimately falling by the wayside on September 30 the following year – 'The King Of Four-Strokes' had gone.

When one talks about Meguro, it's almost certainly the Z that springs to mind. This is the Z7 of April 1956 vintage, its 498cc (82mm x 94mm) single-cylinder engine developing 20bhp at 4400rpm, which was enough to give the 204kg (449lb) machine a top speed of 75mph (120kph).

The Junior S7 (a 248cc ohv single, with a bore and stroke of 65mm x 75mm) was introduced in January 1960 alongside the 123cc CA/CAS pairing. The CA had a regular exhaust system, while the CAS had a fashionable raised one.

Inside pages from the E3 catalogue, printed in the summer of 1958.

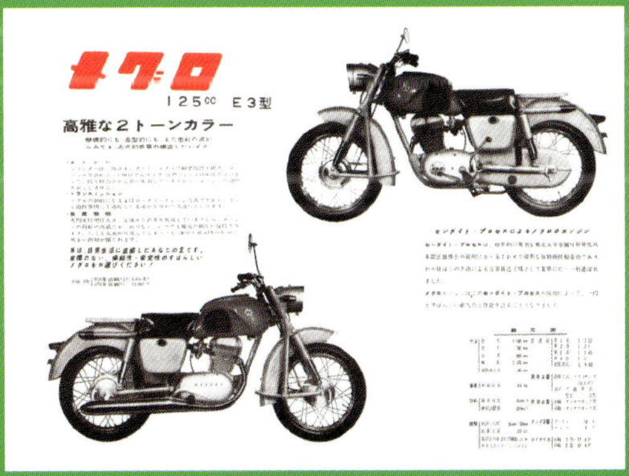

The traditional Meguro tank badge, with an 'M' for Meguro above a 'W' for Works. Kawasaki later modified it, replacing the 'MW' element with the Kawasaki kawa symbol.

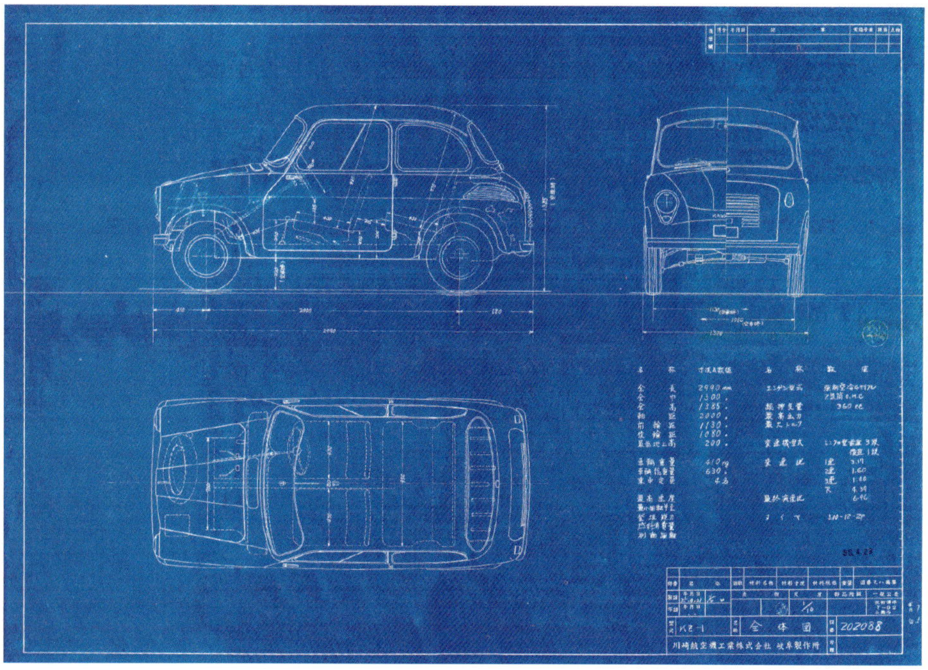

LEFT AND BELOW Blueprint for the KZ-1, dated April 1960, and a finished prototype. Yoji Hamawaki was appointed project leader on the KZ-1 project.

A KAWASAKI AUTOMOBILE

Kawasaki Jidosha Sales Ltd joined forces with Meguro (see sidebar) in August 1961 to handle sales of motorcycles, ultimately leading to the foundation of Kawasaki-Meguro Manufacturing at the end of 1962 before Kawasaki Aircraft took complete control and consigned the Meguro name to the history books. But before any of that happened, the Kawasaki Jidosha Sales Ltd business (Kawasaki Auto Sales in English) had a fascinating background story attached to it – a story that not only makes sense of the automotive bias in the company moniker, but also fills the gaps in the jigsaw puzzle that helps create Kawasaki's motorcycle timeline, and the train of thought behind it.

Part of the reason for the decline in domestic motorcycle sales was the dawn of the car era in Japan, with things set to get harder after the Japanese government proposed a new set of rules to encourage makers to field small, reasonably-priced vehicles better in tune with the times. These machines, with a maximum engine displacement of 360cc, were the first generation of Kei-cars – a breed that survives in Japan to this day, albeit with a 660cc limit.

Kawasaki was keen to get in on the act, so the bus-building department at Gifu was commissioned to produce a body for a four-seater Kei sedan (duly named the KZ-1) in 1959, with one-fifth scale and full-size clays made before

BELOW An amazing 1961 prototype spawned by the KZ project, with a canopy roof (an idea Toyota was also playing with) and narrow rear track. With cars no longer considered a commercially viable option, however, Kawasaki's management had no choice but to embrace the production of motorcycles worthy of the Kawasaki name.

BELOW The Kawasaki Pet M5 moped (left) pictured with the B7 and a Kawasaki 47G-2A helicopter, made under licence from Bell. The M5 had a 49cc engine, while a 53cc B53 version was sold alongside it from mid-1962. There was actually another moped built at Akashi at this time called the Taff, for heavy-duty use; 13,015 Taffs of various types were made for the Iseki concern during 1961 and 1962, with the PA-50 being the most popular model. Kawasaki also made a huge amount of agricultural and commercial diesel engines for Iseki.

running prototypes with glassfibre panels started the test cycle. At the same time, a 356cc two-cylinder power-unit (KZ-360-E1) was developed under Mitsuru Nakajima and aero-engine man Seiji Yamada at the Akashi works. With a 62mm x 59mm bore and stroke, and an 8.0:1 c/r, the sohc four-stroke engine produced 17bhp at 6000rpm; later versions gave 18bhp.

By all accounts, early KZ prototypes displayed promise, but sales outlets were considered a problem. Thoughts regarding the use of the Isuzu network (given Kawasaki's links with Isuzu commercials) were mooted, but Isuzu was already making its own cars at this time – helping a supplier is one thing, but helping a competitor is something completely different, of course. Then, with sales of the Subaru 360 really taking off and the arrival of machines like the Mazda R360 and Mitsubishi 500, plus others waiting in the wings, Kawasaki's beancounters became nervous and ultimately put a stop to the project in mid-1962 before the outside world ever got to hear about it.

In the meantime, Kawasaki displayed its latest 1961 season bikes at the 1960 Tokyo Show, including the Meihatsu 125 New Ace (powered by the two-stroke KB-6AS unit), the Kawasaki B7 (using a fresh B7E engine), and the 49cc two-stroke Kawasaki Pet M5 (project code XKB102, powered by a new M-type powerplant) to try and take on the might of Honda and Suzuki in the lucrative moped arena.

While production of the New Ace had started on August 1, 1960 in Tokyo, before the factory 24 area was completed, both Kawasaki machines were built at the newly-opened plant extension at Akashi, which ultimately had a capacity of 6000 units per month, although only 16,412 M5 and B7 models were built in 1961. Instead of sales increasing, a worse scenario followed, as the moped boom had pretty much peaked. Indeed, while there were 15 makers producing these small machines as 1962 dawned in Japan, only seven were left in the game in 1963. At least Kawasaki's B53 was a success, with 5971 built in 1962 before the figures started dropping off sharply. If nothing else, this highlighted how fashion-led the industry was.

As for the B7, it was found to have several problems relating to the frame, hurting potential sales and costing the

Various views of Kawasaki B7 production and testing, as well as the 123cc B7E engine line (note the oil filler, something not found on the KB-series units), en route to dealerships via a covered wagon, and the finished product. With production starting on January 30, 1961, the Meihatsu New Ace-based B7 was the first bike to carry the Kawasaki brand name. The two-wheeler factory (the specialized site 24) was duly expanded in September 1961, showing Kawasaki's commitment to motorcycles by this stage of the proceedings.

BELOW Away from the motorcycles, Kawasaki was involved in all manner of interesting projects, such as this 1962 monorail system built in conjunction with Lockheed and five other Japanese companies. Kawasaki was a key player in the development and manufacture of the magnificent Shinkansen bullet train, too, which entered service in 1964.

company dearly in claims to put things right. In fact, looking at the production figures, there were more B8s made than B7s in 1962, despite the former not coming on line until the autumn. In addition, there was also a new law passed making it easier to import motorcycles from April 1961, which would also have made a dent in sales totals.

Ironically, the Meguro odyssey was not an easy way out either, as the Meguro network was not as strong as first expected, and it's also fair to say that the engineers at Kawasaki were far from impressed with Meguro technology. This gave the new men attached to the department a few headaches, but also provided them with a first class lesson on how to build better machines in the future. In many ways, it was a situation that the late great Dr Frederick Lanchester would have approved of – looking at what was wrong with a competitor's wares rather than simply copying the good bits. There was also a limited appeal problem to overcome, as Japanese buyers were more likely to buy European or American brands when it came to the big stuff, and all told, Kawasaki held only two per cent of market share in 1963.

It was a dire situation, with exports already a crucial factor in a maker's survival (the American market for Japanese bikes was absolutely huge, offsetting the decline in sales at home, and allowing a few – such as Bridgestone and Yamaguchi – to linger in the States long after they quit the domestic market), but Kawasaki had no links established abroad, and the racing side – an important PR tool – was only just getting off the ground, even then in a very small way. With the stillborn KZ project scuttling another plan, and other business arenas either being long-term investments or not bestowing their potential, it was time to rethink again.

BELOW The 130,000 yen B8 (seen here on the Akashi production lines) was in many ways more important than the B7, for this 11bhp machine, with its pressed steel backbone frame and a new air-cooled single-cylinder B8E two-stroke engine (still sporting a familiar 53mm x 56mm bore and stroke to give 123cc), was the first to be designed from the ground up by Kawasaki engineers. Introduced in October 1962, the B8 project was led by Hiroyuki Matsumoto.

LEFT A useful catalogue from the tail-end of 1963, with the B8M and B8T variations illustrated. The B8 Touring version was sold in America from August 1963, and made it into the home market line-up a few months later. The Meguro pairing looked decidedly antiquated by this time.

BELOW Japan, like America, was being gripped by a scrambling boom. On May 19, 1963, Kawasaki won the first big MFJ motocross event held in Hyogo Prefecture, taking the first six places in the 125cc Class with modified B8 machines. The B8M was introduced as a production replica in October 1963, with a red tank being used to commemorate the company's victory, although it could not be used on the road.

Thankfully, in retrospect at least, Kawasaki Aircraft boss Kimiyo Nagano (a long-serving member of the company, appointed President at the end of 1961) stood by the two-wheelers with certain provisos – one of which was a move towards motorcycles that could guarantee true Kawasaki-level quality. In October 1963, Nagano called for an end to all the squabbling and infighting, telling his workers there was no option but to draw a line in the sand and move forward behind bikes like the all-Kawasaki B8 and new machines in the pipeline. Realising there were no easy shortcuts, this was the full-blooded commitment that was required to put Kawasaki motorcycles on the world stage, and thanks to the in-depth strength of engineering and character within the ranks, success was just around the corner ...

2 THE EARLY W-SERIES MOTORCYCLE

Having treated the motorcycle business almost as a sideline – and often a most frustrating one at that – at last, Kawasaki was now fully committed to two-wheelers. Thanks to President Nagano's declaration at the end of 1963, there would be no more half-hearted attempts, pure and simple. With a newfound conviction running throughout the ranks, the bikes that followed were more than worthy of an aircraft maker ...

This picture from 1963 of the Akashi factory shows the rapid expansion of the site during the early-1960s, with more building being added on the coastal side nearest the camera, as well as beyond the main office block. The first CKD bike kits were shipped out to DELSA in the Philippines during December 1963, incidentally.

The B8, built according to the requirements of users, was proof – if ever it were needed – that Kawasaki had the know-how to create a good bike. The problem was catching up with the likes of Honda and Suzuki, which had a huge range of machines and an equally huge sales network through which to distribute them. These manufacturers also had the American market sorted, and even Yamaha (Japan's third largest bike maker) had established a US office early on, so this was another arena in which Kawasaki would have to play catch-up if it was to rise above the bloodbath of the early sixties, which hardly any of the Japanese motorcycle manufacturers were able to pull through from.

The casualty list just kept on growing in the Land of the Rising Sun, with only the very strongest of makers managing to survive. While the Meguro marque was allowed to fade away, Tohatsu (Tokyo Hatsudoki) had fallen by the wayside in more dramatic fashion by 1964, as had other influential makers such as Miyata and Pointer. Others restricted their two-wheeler activities to the US market: Hodaka (the successor of the failed Yamaguchi brand) and Marusho, which started life badged as the Lilac in Japan. Bridgestone would also continue selling bikes in the States only, but limped on in Japan longer than the others, finally giving up on the home market in 1966.

RIGHT Production of the B8 Touring model, which helped kick off Kawasaki's export drive to the States. A packing area was duly opened next to site 24 at Akashi for export crating prior to shipping at the end of 1964.

BELOW RIGHT The Kawasaki stand at an Osaka trade fair held in the spring of 1964. In the front row, we can see a Meguro S8 Junior, a Meguro K1P (a bike developed for the police, with a revival of its fortunes thanks to the Tokyo Olympics) and a strict Kawasaki B8, distinguished by a black front mudguard and solo seat. In the background, we have a B8M scrambler, a B8T (with a chrome mudguard and pillion seat) and a Kawasaki Pet B53 moped.

It all seemed rather at odds with the buoyant atmosphere at home, with the Tokyo Olympics and the first bullet train service starting. Ironically, this may have been part of the problem. Wages kept increasing rapidly, with the national average going up from 260,000 yen a year in 1960, to 450,000 yen in 1965, at a time when a bowl of noodle soup was around 150 yen, and the average magazine just 50 yen. All of a sudden, cars became an affordable object of desire, and motorbike sales fell as a result, leaving only the fittest in the game – basically those with strong sales outlets in America and Europe.

Indeed, by 1966, between them, Honda, Suzuki, Yamaha and Kawasaki now accounted for 95 per cent of domestic market sales (Bridgestone made up the rest). This situation would have seemed unthinkable only a decade earlier, but at least with Honda specializing in four-stroke engines, Suzuki in two-stroke technology, and Kawasaki and Yamaha having their own appeal, this avoided a direct clash in the showrooms. This may be rushing ahead, but it does at least illustrate that even though Kawasaki's production figures were rising year-on-year (from 19,625 units, including the Taff line, in 1962, to 23,252 in 1963, then 25,275 and 58,682 in 1965), the odds were hardly in the company's favour, and its future was almost entirely dependent on the quality and desirability of the products it was able to field over the next couple of seasons.

A FRESH START

With the benefit of hindsight, the decision by Nagano was a monumental one, although Kawasaki was still new to the motorcycle game in reality, as it had relied on others in several areas of manufacturing for many years, and indeed, the last vestiges of Meguro design elements (and Meihatsu, for that matter, albeit to a lesser extent) were still to be found in Kawasaki machines at the time of Nagano's announcement. Slowly but surely, thanks to people like Teruaki Yamada (an ex-engine design team member who'd taken over from Tetsuro Takahashi once the bike business got under way as a serious thing), more and more 'real' Kawasakis started to take shape ...

In the meantime, production of the B8T (with 'T' standing for Touring) began in February 1964 – a luxury version of the strict B8, with the same 123cc engine but

BELOW The B8S, officially known as the '150 B8S,' which came with an electric (cell) starter, with a kickstart provided as a back-up. Beyond it, we can see the thoroughly modern Kawasaki J1 with a rotary four-speed transmission, which entered production in November 1964. Within a few months, orders for the various J1 series models were up to 3000 units a month, with the factory struggling to keep up with demand. In many ways, it was the first Kawasaki success story, although it should be noted that the B8 run amounted to 38,595 units in the end, so could also be considered fairly successful.

BELOW The 250cc 'Kawasaki-Meguro' SG and SGT grades.

a number of cosmetic modifications aimed at making the machine more attractive. At 140,000 yen, it was 10,000 yen more expensive than the bike on which it was based.

Customer requests for something with more power led to the launch of the Kawasaki B8S in the summer of 1964, its two-stroke single-cylinder engine having a bigger 58mm bore to increase the base unit's displacement from 123cc to 148cc. This increased power output from 11bhp to 12.5bhp, taking the top speed up from 62mph (100kph) to 71mph (114kph) as a result, while there was also a useful improvement in low- and mid-range torque. Priced the same as the B8T, the four-speed B8S would duly go on to be the main line for export markets, at least for a little while, as the model was discontinued in 1966 alongside the B8 and B8T, as well as the limited run B8TR, which was basically an export only hybrid with a B8-type body combined with B8M suspension parts and wheels.

Next up was an interesting touring model called the Kawasaki 250 Meguro SGT, which went into production in September 1964, becoming Kawasaki's first complete four-stroke motorcycle to be made at Akashi along the way. Based on a Meguro prototype (ironic, given that the lines started rolling in the same month as the Meguro concern

LEFT The main gate at the Akashi works, captured on film at around the same time as the K2 was making its debut.

BELOW LEFT The Kawasaki 500 Meguro K2 of 1965 vintage. Some early catalogue images showed a machine very similar to the K1, although this bike has the lighting one more readily associates with the later model.

officially died), this short-lived four-speed machine was powered by an air-cooled 248cc ohv single that gave 18bhp at 7000rpm. Three months later, the company released the Kawasaki 250 Meguro SG (or 250 SG in export markets), which had the same 248cc (66mm x 72.6mm) four-stroke engine as SGT, but a completely different frame surrounding it, borrowed from the Meguro S8 Junior. The SG managed to limp on until the end of 1969, but was totally outdated by then.

In the meantime, the J1 (known as the '85 Standard' in Japan, where it was priced at 76,000 yen) was released just before the SG went to market, sporting a brand new 81.5cc two-stroke single that gave 7.5bhp at 6800rpm. The air-cooled J1E unit was designed to lean forward, following the frame profile that much better, but more importantly, it featured rotary-disc valve induction – the first Kawasaki engine to have this arrangement, which was far more efficient than a traditional piston-port system, and allowed the engineers at Akashi to make serious progress in the smaller capacity arena. Soon after the strict J1 hit the marketplace, J1T (85 Touring) and J1TR (85 Trail) versions were added to the line-up, with their fashionable high-mount exhausts, as well as an 88cc J1M scrambler, and, from the summer of 1965, the J1L and J1TL with the 'superlube' automatic oil injection system that eliminated the need for owners to pre-mix oil with fuel. There was also a J1D (Deluxe) with an electric starter built from 1966, plus a J1TRL, with J1 production finally ending in 1968.

Kawasaki launched a new line of small bikes in 1965 called the M10 and M11. Japan had introduced new rules on mopeds way back in 1961, restricting speeds and banning pillion passengers. All domestic makers got around this by marketing a slightly bigger capacity version of their tiddler models, with the M10 having a 49cc engine and the M11 (which actually came out before the M10) a 52cc lump, for instance.

At the other extreme, after a 1964 Tokyo Show debut, the 496cc Meguro K2 replaced the original K model in March 1965, with the K2P variant made for the police force following in due course, after 12 prototypes were built for testing in 1964. While the Meguro K1 dry-sump ohv twin was basically a direct copy of the BSA A7 unit (albeit a well-built one, though, impressing its designer Edward Turner for one!), the Kawasaki engineers managed to increase peak power a fraction, but the torque curve was completely different, still delivering 1000rpm beyond the K1's peak for unruffled progress. They also improved the lubrication system and tightened tolerances to enhance quality and build consistency for the K2, resulting in an incredibly smooth powerplant that shared only 26 parts with its predecessor. The frame was basically carried over, but gained an extra

RIGHT The 85 J1TL (left) and B1L in export guise. The latter model was basically a combination of the home market B1 and B1T specifications.

BELOW A fascinating photograph of a K2 prototype for the US market. Exports were eyed quite seriously at one point, but the 295,000 yen tourer was never sold abroad in the end, after a sample was found lacking against BSA and Triumph rivals. A K3 proposal, fitted with a powerful ohc engine, never made it past the 'on-paper' stage, but the Meguro X650 project that followed eventually led to the launch of the W1.

bracing piece at the rear to enhance its overall stiffness. A new tank badge was used on the K2s, and the distinctive offside timing cover casting was given a 'Kawasaki' logo in place of the 'Meguro' one (in katakana rather than Roman lettering), both moves highlighting Kawasaki's input in the new bike's development.

According to Kawasaki's official records, only 435 K2s were built, along with 641 K2P police bikes. Almost 3000 K1 variants had been sold following the model's 1960 Tokyo Show debut, by comparison, with around a third being police motorcycles. However, with other domestic makers disappearing fast, the K-series was basically the only Japanese-built big bike available at the time.

No sooner had the little M10 been launched, than the B8's replacement – the similar-looking B1 series – went on the production line. On sale from the end of 1965, the four-speed B1T (or 125 Touring as it was known in the domestic market) had rotary-disc valve induction, boosting power up to 13bhp. The B1T had a raised exhaust system, by the way, and one had to wait until the end of the year with the release of the strict B1 (or 125 Standard) to get a regular muffler arrangement and a more traditional suspension setup. Models with automatic lubrication were added in 1966, giving the B1L and B1TL grades. While the 125 Touring disappeared in 1969, the B1 continued into the 1976 season; even then, the B1 lived on in spirit via the KC125.

October 1965 saw the release of the F1 and F1 Trail models, which were basically lightly modified B8s with the engine bored out to give 169cc and 17bhp. This really was pushing the two-stroke to the limit of its design, but, from the spring of 1966, the F1 pairing was superceded by an F2 range, including an F2TL and F2TRL. The F2 continued into 1969, but the F2TR gave way to a fleeting but decidedly more modern F3 variant at the end of 1967, a model known as the Bushwhacker in the States.

Early 1966 brought some more J1-based variants, including the C1 (120 Standard), with a bigger bore and stroke than the 47mm x 47mm dimensions used on the J1 to give a 115cc displacement, and the D1, with a 52mm bore to provide a new albeit shortlived 99cc model. There was also a Touring version of the latter with a raised exhaust, as well as a Deluxe version of the C1, equipped with a self-starter, plus the obligatory 'superlube' grades.

While all this was going on, a new engine line had been completed at the site 24 building by January 1965, and at last, motorcycle production hit the factory's then maximum capacity of 6000 units a month by the middle of the year (total 1965 CY production hit almost 60,000 units – a huge increase on the 5414 posted in 1960), keeping the threat from an axe hanging over the bike project once more until financially successful lines like the A1 parallel-twin wiped

Japanese advertising from early 1966.

away any remaining fears once and for all, when monthly production figures would hit the 9000 mark.

Planning for the future was also becoming more evident, with greater streamlining of operations (such as moving the paint shop and welders to be closer to the production line) and, in gradual steps, the greater standardization of parts. If the Kawasaki Aircraft Co (or KAC) was to compete with its compatriots effectively, these areas would become increasingly important from a business angle, especially if the larger production volumes anticipated were to be accomplished with a worthwhile degree of profitability. At the same time, the final traces of Meihatsu and Meguro disappeared with 120 shops being established as a brand new Kawasaki network. While it was a bit too late to cash-in on the boom years, and it was always going to be hard competing with established concerns like Honda and Suzuki (who were also nimble in the boardroom – useful in a fast-moving environment like the bike world), but the progress was there and of a noteworthy level, too.

In addition, there was the first official works entry in a GP race during this time – a bold move that would duly see Kawasaki begin a proper racing campaign, with several European rounds challenged in 1966, including the legendary Isle of Man TT. Results would take a while to come through, which was hardly surprising given the amount of catching up Kawasaki had to do in this most competitive of arenas, but it was another necessary step forward if the marque was ever to become recognized as a serious player. For once, Kawasaki would have a little luck on their side, with the FIM annoying Honda and Suzuki to the point that they eventually withdrew from racing, thus allowing Kawasaki to steal the limelight that much easier (even though Yamaha would have a say in the Japanese racing bike wars). We'll come to that particular story later on, but at least we can see that the company was definitely moving in the right direction, trying its best to enhance its image for enthusiasts.

Competition review: the early days

Although the J1 had provided Kawasaki with an ideal little racer since the spring of 1965, the firm's early competition success centred on scrambling, which was a booming sport both in Japan and abroad as the company began to make serious inroads into the motorcycling arena. However, the focus quickly moved to the more glamorous world of larger-displacement road racers. And why not? Every maker worth its salt had gained or at least solidified its reputation on the tracks, so it was an obvious route for Kawasaki to take, even if it did look like a daunting journey. Thankfully, the uphill struggle that would have undoubtedly faced the company was tempered with all the upheaval in FIM ranks at the time, reducing the technological (and budgetary) jump that others had on Kawasaki, having been in the racing game for so much longer. The timing was definitely right ...

Rare catalogue image for the A1-R road racer.

As well as an attractive 250cc production-based racer called the A1-R (on sale from December 1966), Kawasaki campaigned a 125cc twin that had made its debut at the Japanese Grand Prix in 1965. Sadly, the Suzuka event was not kind to Kawasaki, with all three machines retiring. For 1966, the 32bhp water-cooled disc-valve 125s were improved, gaining an eight-speed gearbox, and Kawasaki also secured the services of Toshio Fujii, who'd ridden for Suzuki in the previous year. Considering Fujii was given a single bike and one mechanic – nothing else! – he was doing well holding sixth in the West German GP (the season's second round at Hockenheim), but had to settle for a DNF mark in the end. Retirements followed in East Germany and Czechoslovakia, but the Isle of Man TT was worse, for the rider died following a heavy crash, and the team was not seen again until the Japanese GP at Fuji Speedway. Kawasaki now had ex-Honda man, Naomi Taniguchi (who could throw a spanner as well as ride hard) in its fledgling race department, with testing being his main job, and the legendary Ernst Degner was signed to race. Unfortunately, a chain breaking in practice ruled him out for the actual race, but ultimately Ken Araoka was seventh, Dave Simmonds eighth, and Chris Vincent a distant tenth in the 125cc category.

Although still off the pace, at least the 1966 season had ended with a glimmer of hope. Despite the FIM's changes to the rules that wiped out Kawasaki's V4 before it was able to show its potential, things would continue in the right direction in 1967 after Kawasaki signed Simmonds (who'd started his career on Tohatsu tiddlers before moving up to bigger Honda steads), loaning him a 125cc twin and an A1-R. The results of this signing were not obvious straight away, but after Honda and Suzuki withdrew from the Grand Prix circuit before the 1968 season was due to begin, Simmonds slowly but surely began to shine in the 125cc category, then being dominated by Yamaha's British pair, Phil Read and Bill Ivy.

In America, Yoji Hamawaki and Sam Tanegashima displayed an A1 prototype at Daytona in 1966, and were encouraged to start racing by several influential people, including Jack DuPont. The 250 tested by *Cycle World* in its December 1966 issue duly became a production racer, prepared by Dave Kimball for the factory. It won first time out at Willow Springs with Jimmy Deehan at the controls, and won a few other races, too. The most important thing was it led to the A1-R, which raced at Daytona in 1967, and laid the foundations for other production-based racers to follow. For the record, there was a W1-R prototype built, as well as a W1S-R fitted with a sidecar. Neither saw any serious competition, but it's interesting to note their existence ...

The twin-cylinder 125cc water-cooled racer of 1966, with a close-up of the 40bhp 125cc V4 two-stroke engine used in what was basically the same frame, although the latter was only ever ridden in anger at the non-championship 1967 Singapore Grand Prix due to a change in the FIM rules on the use of multi-cylinder engines.

A couple of race-prepared A7s running in the 1967 Japanese GP, with Masahiro Wada on the left, and Ken Araoka taking the inside line. Wada was the top Kawasaki finisher in the 350cc category on the day, taking fourth.

The A7-R was added as a 350cc production racer in time for the 1969 season, joining a revised A1-RA for the 250cc category. The two-stroke A7-R was powered by a 338cc twin, putting its 53bhp down through a five-speed gearbox (this is the A7-RS with a modified frame, by the way). Note the signature Kawasaki Racing Green paintwork – a colour Rollin 'Molly' Sanders convinced America's Hamawaki and Masek to go along with, changing the corporate track image from red to lime green as a result. As a matter of interest, 'Molly' was also responsible for Yamaha's yellow and black colouring that would last a generation.

The first signs of Kawasaki in America, with a one-third page advert from the June 1964 issue of *Cycle World*. The bikes are the 'Trojan Magnum Super Sport' and B8M, although the B8T (ultimately sold with Omega badging) would be the first Kawasaki to hit US shores. Kay actually supplied a B8T (or Omega Sports Special 125) to *Cycle World* for test. It stated: "We have become accustomed to nice finishes on small-displacement, inexpensive Japanese motorcycles, but the Omega sets a new standard in this regard." The magazine was also impressed by the smoothness of the engine and the ride quality.

CALIFORNIA DREAMIN'

If Kawasaki's entry into the realm of motorcycles had been far from easy and straightforward, its American odyssey was not much different, fraught with hardships, trial and error of the kind simple bullet points on a timeline fail to illustrate. Again, this would be a fascinating story to tell on its own but, for the time being, we shall at least illustrate how Kawasaki came to make a mark on the US marketplace.

The American market was truly huge, with machines being shipped over from various parts of postwar Europe at a pace that some makers could only just keep up with. Then, of course, Honda arrived on the scene, and the complexion of the playing field simply changed overnight. What was interesting was that Honda, Yamaha and Suzuki (the latter joining the fray quite late compared to the other pair it should be noted) all had their own corporate offices in California to punt their wares, which was a luxury afforded to few of the import brands. For instance, at the start of 1964, Norton was handled by Joseph Berliner of the Berliner Motor Corporation of New Jersey, who also looked after Ducati, NSU and Motobi models were imported by West Valley Cycle Sales of California, MV Agusta, Parilla and Bianchi lines by Cosmopolitan Motors of Philadelphia, BMW by Butler & Smith and Flanders, Gilera by C&N Enterprises, Zanella by Standard Atlantic Corporation, and Velocette by the MC Supply Company. Only BSA and Triumph (and perhaps Jawa) could really rival the Japanese when it came to brand representation, and even these famous marques were covered by independent firms on the west coast. In other words, there was nothing unusual in having an outside party handle things, and trading companies were the way Japan did things as a rule of thumb, the latter acting as middlemen in order to collect a cut of the proceeds for as little effort as possible. But, as the author's old friend Yutaka Katayama quickly concluded on a recce trip for Nissan, if one was to succeed in the States, one needed a base there, offering all the back-up a customer would expect in a product's native land.

If one ignores the small shipments sent to Hawaii in 1963 via the Jupitor Trading Co and brought about by an earlier Meguro distribution deal, Kawasaki joined some of the smaller Japanese makers in appointing a private importer to handle US sales in order to get a foot in the door. In this case, it was the Ken Kay Distributing Co of Sherman Way, North Hollywood, CA, who'd actually looked after Suzuki's distribution in its early days in the States.

The first signs of this new alliance – with the Ataka Trading Co lurking quietly in the background as his supplier from KAC, as Kay was not supplied directly – appeared in the June 1964 issue of *Cycle World*, although the Kawasaki and Meguro brand names were kept in the background – Kay preferred to use his own Omega badging, announced alongside the Trojan nameplate. A similar advert was placed in the following issue before a big splash in August, introducing the Omega Sports Special 125. The 175cc Trojan Magnum Super Sport, based on an Italian machine, had been displayed at the Daytona International Motorcycle Show to kick Kay's latest venture off, while the Omega was basically a B8T, and became the first Kawasaki to hit the shores of mainland America. At $435 (with whitewall tyres and a chrome luggage rack listed as options), it was priced roughly the same as the Yamaha YA-6, also sporting a 125cc lump, and was duly joined by the $550 Omega Kangaroo Scrambler 125, better known as the B8M. This was a good move, as MX machines were all the rage in the States at the time.

Looking through old magazines, it's clear that while a traditional market still existed in the States, interest was definitely rising in off-roaders (giving a welcome financial boost for the likes of Jawa, Montesa, Bultaco, Greeves and Cotton), and scooter sales were taking off, too. Adverts for the likes of the Lambretta, Vespa, Rabbit, Bridgestone tiddlers (sold through Rockford) and MV Agusta Chicco may have been unthinkable only a few years earlier, but even Harley-Davidson was downsizing, offering bikes like the Pacer and the Topper scooter for its diehard customers. This move towards smaller engines also opened up the way for 50cc bikes, which were no longer a laughing stock in American eyes due to their well-documented success in the racing arena.

By the tail-end of summer 1964, Ken Kay was listing no less than 33 Omega dealers in his advertising, which increased to 56 by the start of autumn, although he was still pushing himself as a Suzuki parts supplier as well, and the small adverts that followed pointed to a lack of a proper budget – the 'Big Three' (for Kawasaki could hardly be deemed to be in the same league in terms of sales, as Honda was building around 1,450,000 units a year at this time, with Suzuki around 340,000 and Yamaha 245,000, and a total of 868,756 exports accounting for a large chunk of those numbers) were always taking full-page spreads as an absolute minimum in the leading Stateside magazines, with an extensive range to peddle, too, rather than just a handful of B8-based models, duly augmented by a number of J1 variants once they started filtering through from March 1965 onwards. Only in the second half of 1965 was the brand represented with decent advertising, but by then, KAC was placing its own adverts, and Ken Kay was seen cutting back again – in retrospect, a welcome move perhaps, for Kay was known to be struggling to keep up with his payments.

According to Kawasaki records, an office was set up in Los Angeles in October 1964, although it was actually little more than a desk at the K-Line Shipping building, with ex-Tohatsu man Fred Suginuma watching over Ken Kay's progress from the start of the following year. Things didn't really start happening until the middle of 1965, when KAC struck a deal with four trading companies: Nissho Trading supplied Skokie International (covering 24 states, on the east coast as far as Ohio and the southern states across to New Mexico); Naigai Boeki tied up with Waner & Waner of Chicago, who in turn supplied Kawasaki Midwest (KMW) to service Michigan, Indiana, Ohio, Kentucky and Tennessee, as well as Fox Distribution, who looked after Minnesota, Wisconsin, Iowa, Illinois and Missouri; Naigai Boeki also supplied Masek Auto Supply Stores, who served the seven states above New Mexico and Oklahoma (and also held some of the first service schools), Joe Dobbins, who controlled Oregon and Washington, and General Implement of Idaho; Ataka Trading continued to look after Ken Kay's east coast operation, while Yoshiro Fujimura's Jupitor Trading was the middleman for Wholesale Motors, servicing Hawaii. Only Alaska was left out of the picture.

Following a meeting held four months earlier, further commitment was made in August 1965, when a proper office was established in Chicago for motorcycle sales and spares (interestingly, a lack of spares back-up had been one of the main complaints in consumer feedback – an important point considering 1800 bikes had been sold Stateside in June 1965 alone, along with a further 2400 in the following month), and the first adverts were placed by KAC in enthusiast publications showing the Kawasaki name at the same time.

As far as the Japanese big hitters were concerned, everyone else was based in California, but the thinking behind the location was sound enough, with the west coast saturated and the east coast still relatively untapped, and

BELOW Key people in the Stateside story pictured on a trip to Kyoto. From left to right: Ryozo Iwaki, Dave Mehney (KMW), Alan Masek (RMK, later AKM), and Yoji Hamawaki. Masek was the man who brought local knowledge to the Kawasaki US organization, suggesting model year (MY) changes and other ways in which to increase market share.

BELOW Yoji 'George' Hamawaki (then VP of AKM, and future President of KMC) outside a Skokie dealership with a B8T and B8S beside him. It will be remembered that Hamawaki had been in charge of Kawasaki's abandoned Kei-car project. After a spell in Brazil, he would go on to become a leading light in Kawasaki's motorcycle export drive. Hamawaki left for BMW in 1981, and was later inducted into the Japan Automotive Hall of Fame (JAHFA).

it was also a useful position for distribution to the central, as well as the eastern states. Market research began in earnest from here, leading to the formation of the American Kawasaki Motorcycle Corporation (or AKM) on March 1, 1966, registered at 28 South LaSalle Street in downtown Chicago, followed by a parts warehouse a few miles north of the main office. Ryozo Iwaki (one of the directors at Akashi, and general manager of the motorcycle engine department) was appointed the first President, with Yoji Hamawaki as VP.

While the domestic sales company was renamed Kawasaki Autoby Hanbai (Kawasaki Motorcycle Sales) in February 1966, which was far more suitable than the old 'jidosha' moniker and pointed towards a secure future for the two-wheeler line, beyond the Iwaki-Hamawaki pair, few in America, or anywhere else for that matter, would have been aware that this was quite literally a make or break situation on the future of the bike business – a failure here meant the end of the Kawasaki motorcycle project!

Then things started to get complicated. The Waner & Waner deal fell through due to a shortfall in the agreed sales levels, so AKM took over the Fox Distribution area, and KMW gained greater independence. Meanwhile, the Ataka concern decided it had finally had enough of Ken Kay's financial woes, and pulled the plug in 1966. In November that year, Iwaki duly negotiated a deal that allowed AKM to open its own distribution and dealer network in three of the four states previously handled by Ken Kay (the fourth one, Utah, went to General Implement, who already served Idaho, and would until 1975), in addition to the ex-Fox states. The sales office was then moved to South Main Street in Gardena, CA, with a then young Alan Masek moving across from Nebraska to give a greater level of 'native' knowledge to the operation.

However, further problems came after Osamu 'Sam' Tanegashima was sent by KAC in the early part of 1966 to liaise with the Skokie outfit – a lack of sales (and payments to Nissho Trading) against orders that were far too

BELOW A visit to the ex-World Cycles dealership on Sunset Boulevard in California during 1966. Ken Kay took the place over for a while, when he was responsible for Kawasaki distribution in CA, NV, UT and AZ, and even had it featured in an advert – his last one for Kawasaki as it happens … (Courtesy Y Hamawaki)

BELOW LEFT The first English language brochure for the W1, or 650 W1 to give the bike its full title. The illustration shows the W1 with US-spec lighting.

optimistic (no less than 7000 B8s and J1s were ordered over the three months either side of Christmas 1965) led to the formation of the Eastern Kawasaki Motorcycle Corporation (EKM) in March 1967, taking over the ex-Skokie area via direct (ie. factory to dealer) sales from offices in New Jersey. At least Masek's distribution operation remained much the same, gaining the Rocky Mountain Kawasaki (RMK) moniker along the way, as did Joe Dobbins in the north-west (at least until 1969) and Wholesale Motors of Hawaii.

There was more reshuffling when in January 1968, Texas, New Mexico and Oklahoma were transferred to AKM from EKM (which made sense), but thankfully, the top people in Japan stood by the men in America, giving chance after chance to make things work. Their patience, which must have ran thin on many occasions (especially considering that all Japanese bike sales were seriously down across America in the second half of 1967, with dealers failing to pay and falling by the wayside like lemmings), was finally being rewarded. As it happens, 1968 was a good year for the brand, and the Kawasaki motorcycle would eventually go on to be the giant conglomerate's signature product, largely thanks to bikes like the A1 and the legendary W1 and H1 models, ordered by Hamawaki for the US market. Before we go too far ahead, it's time to look at the W1 in detail …

A NEW BREEZE

It was ironic that the new breeze sweeping through Kawasaki was in fact thanks to an 'olde worlde' bike aimed at challenging Harley-Davidson and the big British machines that dominated the Stateside showrooms in the heavyweight category. The request had come through the sales department following a meeting in the spring of 1965, pointing to a dire need for more leisure-oriented and bigger bikes for the US market, and was – as usual – required yesterday! As such, the motorcycle division chief, Michiharu Tsukamoto, was under great pressure to deliver a new bike as soon as possible, and ultimately many of the proposals for engine improvements had to be discarded due to time concerns. Notwithstanding, a thorough job was done, as one would expect from a strong team with a passion for motorcycles and engineering in general, and the end result was nothing short of a masterpiece, despite early examples

LEFT AND BELOW A couple of early promotional shots for the W1. From this angle, one can see that the characteristic headlight shape found on some of the smaller Kawasakis (Suzuki also used an odd profile for headlight casings to distinguish them from competitors) was dropped in favour of a pure round item, as per the Meguro K2. The indicators on either side of the headlight, similar to those of the K2, illustrate home market lighting regulations, which also dictated the use of a slightly different rear lamp unit. Oddly, indicators were still classed as an option by Japanese law until January 1, 1969, although most makers fitted them anyway.

having their fair share of problems. As we've come to expect, nothing was easy or straightforward, but Kawasaki's men stuck with it and, in doing so, created a legend.

The four-speed 650 W1 sports tourer was announced at the 1965 Tokyo Show (running from October 30 to November 11, and visited by an amazing 1,465,000 people), as what was then Japan's biggest bike, aimed at stealing the limelight from machines like the Honda CB450. Checking through old magazines from the time, one can see that the W1 prototype (developed under the Meguro X650 codename) looked exactly like the K2 illustrated earlier in the book, except for Kawasaki badging on the fuel tank and a bigger engine.

As noted earlier, the Kawasaki engineers modified the Meguro K1 powerplant to a huge extent to create the air-cooled K2 ohv vertical-twin, but for the W1, over 300 parts were carried over from the latter by the small, tight-knit four-stroke engine group, consisting of Gyoichi 'Ben' Inamura (who'd worked on the KZ360 project as a young intern, and later helped refine the Meguro K-series lump), Tadashige Yamada, Takashi Inoue, Toshihiko Suzuki and Ryochi Hashimoto, plus Horimoto and Chatani on the testing side.

There were major differences, though. While the K2 had a bore and stroke of 66mm x 72.6mm to give 496cc, the pair of cylinders were bored out to 74mm to take the displacement up to 624cc. While the same 8.7:1 compression ratio was employed, this 128cc in capacity increase took the maximum power up from 36bhp at 6500rpm (for the K2) up to 50bhp for the W1 in export guise (which used the W1E unit), developed at the same engine speed.

Although the cast iron linerless block looked similar from the outside, the new bore/stroke relationship gave the newcomer a quite different character to the K2. Also, as well

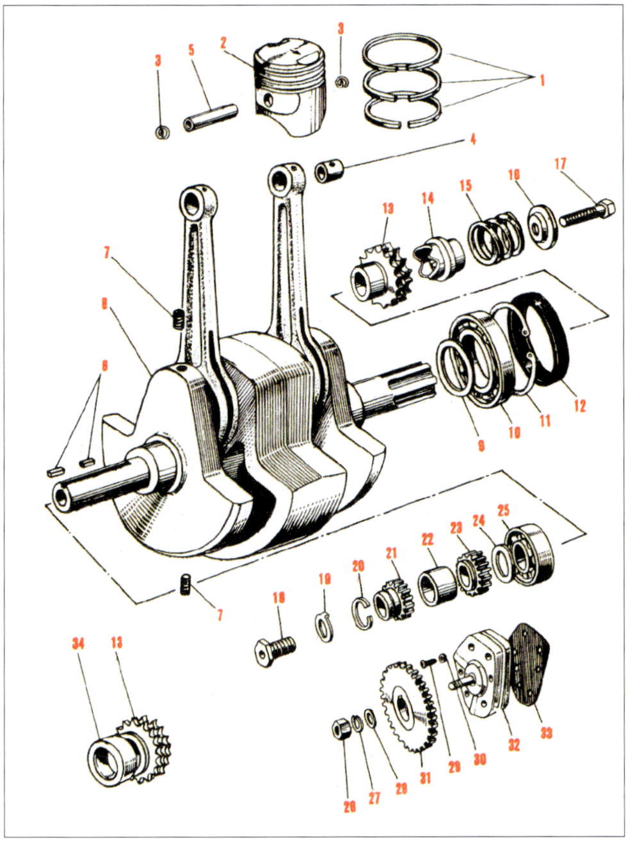

LEFT The bottom-end of the W1 engine, as seen in the parts book.

as extra bolts to hold everything together and increase the rigidity of the unit, a new bottom-end had to be designed to deal with the additional horses, using a combination of a roller bearing at the drive end and a ball bearing at the other, as the needle bearings preferred by the development team would have required three mains instead of the existing two. The crankshaft was different nonetheless, being a built-up crank on the W1 against a forged single piece item on the K2, but this allowed needle bearings to be specified for the conrod big ends at least. This meant the crank and one-piece connecting rods could only be bought as an assembly according to the parts book, but it was a small price to pay for the reduction in friction. The lubrication system was also uprated to cope with the additional stresses caused by the power increase. Both dry and wet sump systems were tested, although the problems associated with early Ks were solved quite easily in the end via fresh oil line routes and a stronger oil pump, allowing the dry sump setup to be retained. Interestingly, the Kawasaki engineers provided a small removable oil filter for the tank to keep dirt from damaging the crank bearings, while a novel crankcase breather system helped stop the bike from leaving its 'calling card' in the form of wet black spots on the road.

An overhead valve arrangement was retained, using a gear-driven camshaft to move the pushrods, and while the exhaust valves were the same diameter as those found in the K2 engine, the inlets were increased in size; a bigger VM31 carburettor was employed as well, with the inlet manifold an integral part of the alloy head casting. The head itself again looked familiar, with the same heavy ribbing found in the block for cooling, and the pair of exhausts exiting from the leading edge corners to flow back, finished with a separate low-mounted muffler on each side of the bike – one pipe for each cylinder. A battery and coil ignition was specified, with the battery charged by a chain-driven dynamo.

The end result of all this effort was an engine with a nice, meaty torque curve until the 5500rpm peak was reached, then it dropped off rapidly, and ran out of steam completely after peak power was hit 1000rpm later. This was not meant to be a manic racer, of course – that was the domain of the two-stroke brigade. The W1 was always going to be happier playing the role of a refined cruiser. However, even in home market 47bhp guise (engine code UKB271, with pilot production starting on March 15, 1966), the W1 was significantly quicker than the K2 over the standing-quarter, despite having the same tyre sizes and gearing that was much the same, with only subtle changes made to the spec sheet to suit the new engine's characteristics.

On the subject of gearing, the W1 kept the K2's separate transmission with a right shift, left brake layout (aping the traditional UK arrangement – the opposite to US and the usual Japanese practice, including that of Kawasaki, although the larger Meguros had used this layout for a number of years, which is hardly surprising given their design roots), although a heavier clutch was employed to deal with the additional power and torque. The shift was arranged so that neutral was at the 'top' of the sequence, followed by first, second, third, and fourth at the 'bottom.'

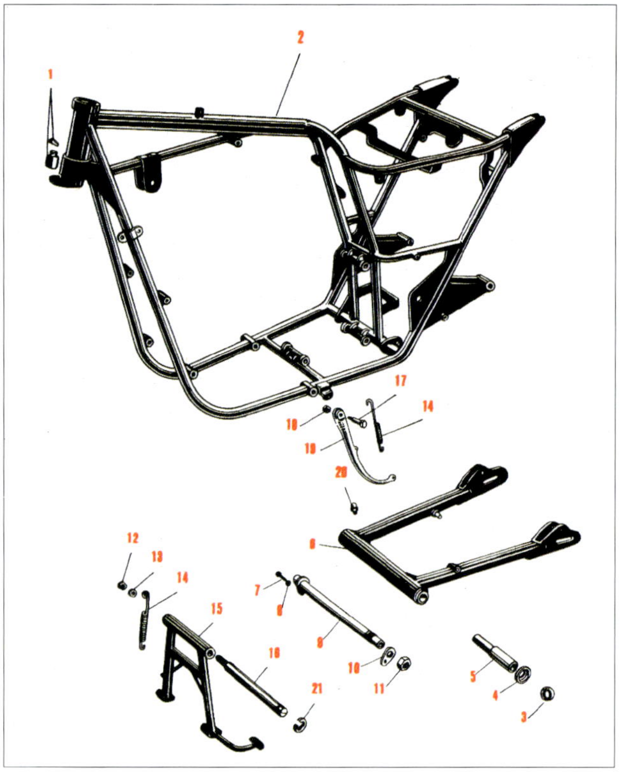

LEFT The W1 frame, made from welded sections of tubular steel.

BELOW The first W1 advert used in the States, dating from July 1966.

OPPOSITE American advertising from the summer of 1966, which provides the reader with a lot more detail than the original ad. Note that the overhead view on the rear page has been printed as a reverse image.

The duplex frame was basically carried over, although the K2 had a slightly longer 1430mm (56.3in) wheelbase than the W1, and the latter also had a new adjustable steering damper and revised front brakes. There were no surprises in the telescopic fork up front and a swing-arm suspension at the back, the drum brakes (with drums made of aluminium alloy sporting iron liners) and 18-inch wheels and tyres – all were familiar fare, even if things like lashings of chrome and rubber bellows on the fork added a touch of modernity into the equation. Toshio Togashi (an ex-Meguro man) looked after the frame and other chassis components, so perhaps the lack of major changes is easily explained.

A number of components were shared with the A1, a bike that had actually been under development longer than the W1, which was something of a rush job. The large round headlight with an integral speedometer (duly calibrated in kph for Japan and mph for most other countries) and tachometer was a good example, along with the fuel tank pressing, even though the final colouring (aimed squarely at contemporary US tastes) made them look quite different at first glance.

Using a percentage of the 55 built in 1965 for promotion purposes, the 650cc bike duly did the rounds on the American show circuit before going on sale there in May 1966, facing up to the threat from machines like the 650 BSAs and Triumphs, as well as the 750 Norton and, to a lesser extent, the racy 650 Laverda. As it happens, Kawasaki's exports had been increasing generally, with a big order from Vietnam for 5000 M10s in 1966, and fresh CKD contracts signed with companies in Taiwan, Thailand, Indonesia, Iran, Pakistan, Nigeria and Columbia. Exports to Europe began officially in the spring of 1967, with the company taking a stand at the Earls Court Show that year, and the racing programme helping to promote the brand in that neck of the woods. The effort was duly rewarded, as 1967 saw income from exports exceed that from domestic

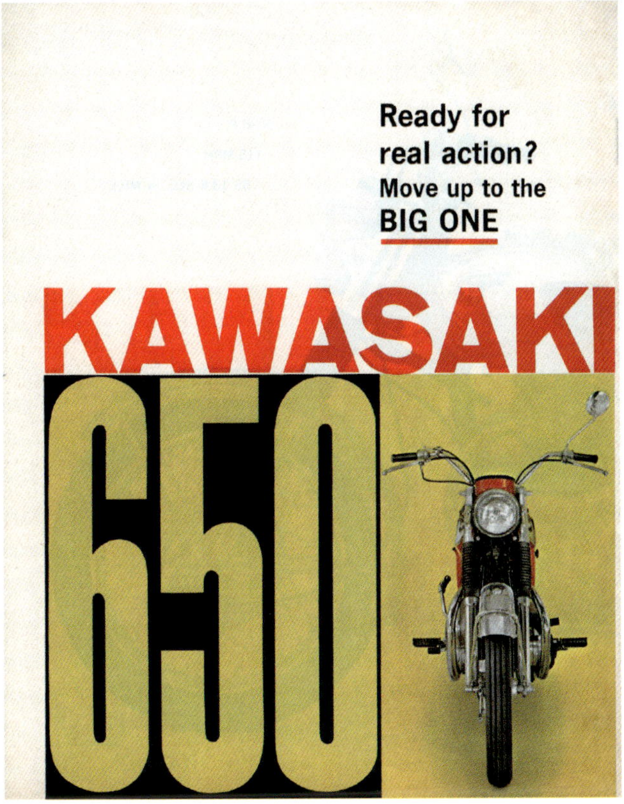
Ready for
real action?
Move up to the
BIG ONE
KAWASAKI
650

JAPAN'S BIGGEST, FASTEST,
MOST POWERFUL MOTORCYCLE!
If you're ready to move up from a 125cc or 250cc, don't go part way. Make the BIG MOVE to the Kawasaki 650, and straddle 50 horses of big, bold, beautiful power in the biggest, fastest and most responsive Japanese motorcycle ever built for the American road!
This thoroughbred of engineering excellence arouses the sporting juices as few things in life can. (Surging a quarter mile from a standing start in less than 14 seconds isn't acceleration, it's exhilaration!) Yet, in conception and design, the Kawasaki 650 is the safest, easiest handling machine of its size in the world.
KAWASAKI AIRCRAFT CO., Ltd., 2860 N. Lincoln Ave., Chicago, Illinois 60657
Main Office: Tokyo, Japan • West Coast Office: Los Angeles, California
ENGINE – 4 stroke, vertical twin, OHV
TRANSMISSION – Forward, 4-speed, foot shift
MAX. HORSEPOWER – 50 hp/6,500 rpm
MAX. SPEED – 115 mph
SS ¼ MILE – 13.8 sec.
COMPRESSION RATIO – 8.7:1
MAX. TORQUE – 40.5 ft. lb./5,500 rpm
BORE X STROKE – 2.91 x 2.89"
WEIGHT – 398 lbs.
DOUBLE LEADING FRONT BRAKE
MANUFACTURED TO EXACTING AIRCRAFT STANDARDS of 1/1000 MILLIMETER TOLERANCES by Kawasaki Aircraft Co., Ltd., one of the world's largest manufacturing complexes and a leader in the challenging world of transportation.
FUN PEOPLE
GO KAWASAKI

KAWASAKI
650
America's New Cross-Town, Cross Country Highway King
• 50 H.P.
• 115 MPH
• SS 13.8 SEC. ¼ MILE

RIGHT The W1 featured on the cover of the August 1966 issue of *Cycle World.*

BELOW The home market W1. Strict W1 colours included Black, Candy Red and Candy Blue, by the way, both at home and abroad.

OPPOSITE An early W1 for the US market, which didn't require front or rear indicators at this time. Note the oil filler in the centre of the oil tank's top edge.

sales (Japan had no less than 64 domestic distributors and 4200 sales outlets at this time!) for the first time since the bike business began.

Meanwhile, the W1 was starting to make an impression in America. Having clocked a 15.6 second standing-quarter with the $1195 machine (against $995 for a 500cc flat-twin Marusho – the only other real Japanese touring bike available at the time, although a good $200 cheaper than a BSA Spitfire Mark III), the August 1966 edition of *Cycle World* noted: "Sheer, blinding speed is not one of the Kawasaki's attributes ... What the Kawasaki does well is medium-speed cruising. The bike is very smooth, and cruises along at 70mph as though it would continue forever. Starting is extremely easy, hot or cold, and it will pull along in traffic without any of the stuttering and stumbling that is characteristic of the 'performance above all' motorcycle. The Kawasaki impressed us as being made with more than the usual care. On balance, a very good motorcycle."

It wasn't all plain sailing, though, for a number of problems took root as a result of rushing to get the model out quickly in the States. Whereas the A1 had been tested extensively in the US environment, highlighting trouble before sales began, the W1 had hardly turned a wheel in America before dealers started taking orders! With rough road use being more prevalent, often at speeds far higher than those witnessed at home, and frame damage led to a number of claims. There were also a lot of complaints about engine vibration, mostly due to overly enthusiastic use, prompting the company to stop selling the W1 in America for a little while, relying on the best-selling A1 and A7 two-stroke models instead. However, modifications were soon applied, and the model was able to ride out the storm, at least for the short-term.

Domestic W1 sales were supposed to start in July 1966, but were ultimately delayed a little due to the early feedback from America. In any case, A1 sales (due to begin in August) took priority in the eyes of the dealers, and indeed, the W1 was initially built to order until sales started to take off. Ironically, given that a) the W1 was designed with export markets in mind and b) big bikes were hardly popular per se in Japan, with only ten or so a month being imported from Europe and America, there was an excellent response from home market buyers, with the bike's character fitting in perfectly with its surroundings and the requirements of its users. A legendary status was guaranteed, but Japanese

KAWASAKI

RIGHT & BELOW RIGHT Range brochure from the summer of 1966, including the W1 and the highly-successful 250cc A1 'Samurai.'

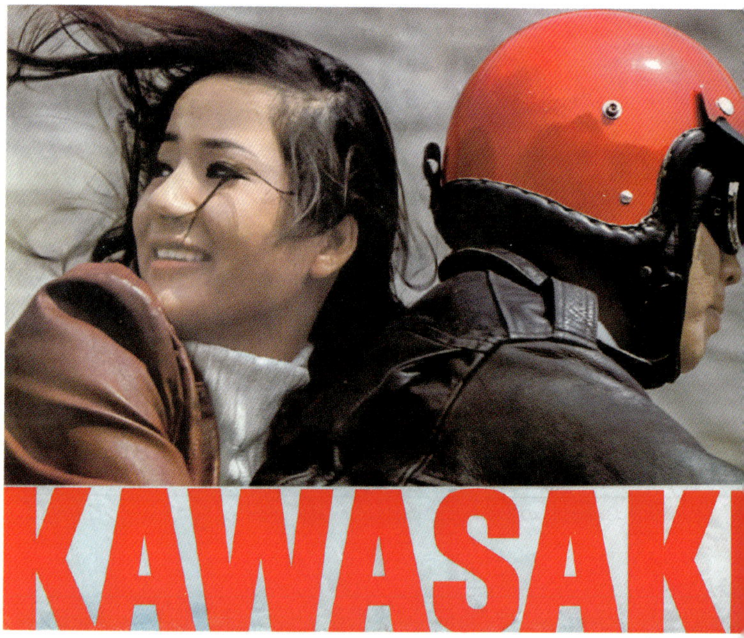

sales would always be small fry, and success can only really be measured in business by a return on investment. Those crucial US sales were an absolute must if the model was to survive. At the same time, this was the company's flagship, so saving face was the only real option ...

Work on refining the W engine began as soon as the W1 was launched, the four-stroke team using engineering journals, reference vehicles (including cars), and old data going back to the Meihatsu and Meguro days. Most of this material was ancient, of course, so the very latest technology was also studied. With reports filtering back from the States as well, not only about problems encountered, but also the desired features US riders sought, the group in charge of the 650's development soon had a concept with which to move forward.

In the meantime, May 1966 saw the release of the 169cc B11TL (175 Touring), a larger-engined version of the B1 equivalent duly followed by a B11L (175 Standard), but also marked the launch of the landmark A1 '250 Sports.' Known as the 'Samurai' abroad, the two-stroke A1 had an air-cooled 247cc twin (53mm x 56mm) with dual carbs and rotary valves, delivering 31bhp at a heady 8000rpm. With a five-speed gearbox and 18-inch tyres, the 145kg (319lb) machine would easily do the ton, and could dismiss the standing-quarter in 15.1 seconds. This was the bike that really put Kawasaki on the map in export markets, and domestic sales were buoyant, too, with home market dealerships beginning to sell the A1 in August.

More bread-and-butter models followed in the shape of the G1 – an 88cc version of the J1 in reality, and destined to take its place in the showrooms over the next year or so. A G1M motocross bike was also launched in March 1967 (replacing the J1M), and a whole string of other variants as per the original J1 line. On the subject of MX machines, the B8M was replaced by the B1M in the summer of 1966, and joined a few months later by a more serious F21M (or 'Scrambler' as it was badged in the States) powered by a 238cc two-stroke single.

BELOW The W1P was announced in July 1966, eventually selling in Japan, America, Australia, Korea and Guatemala. The author has seen a prototype picture with chrome mudguards, but they were painted white by the time orders were being taken. Whatever finish they had, though, they were certainly a lot lighter than the hefty fenders used on the K-series models! One was displayed at the 1966 Tokyo Show, alongside a regular W1 placed in front of a projection screen on rollers, the images reacting to the 'speed' of the bike.

BOTTOM LEFT & RIGHT A rather jolly Japanese language brochure for the 650 W1. The details on the back boast of the bike's rapid standing-quarter time and top speed, and the 47 horses available at the flick of a wrist.

BELOW Kiyoshi Yotsumoto became President of KAC in November 1966 – a key time in Kawasaki's history if it was to succeed going into the seventies. After the 1969 reshuffle, he was named Vice President of the new concern, but was duly elected President of KHI within a few months.

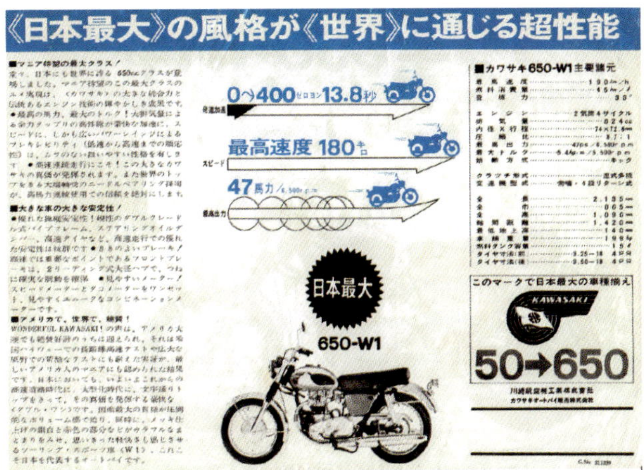

THIS PAGE Japanese range brochure from early 1967, with Kawasaki by now fielding something to suit everyone.

SPORTING PRETENCES

Developed from user feedback, the spring of 1967 brought a flood of sporting models making their debut, many using the 'SS' moniker, which stood for 'street scrambler' according to Kawasaki's sales lingo, even though the link with true MX machines was rather tenuous to say the least. The first of these, featuring a raised exhaust system and a lightweight tubular frame, was the 120 C2SS (or 'Road Runner' abroad), powered by an all-alloy 115cc two-stroke engine with rotary disc induction. There was also a 120 C2TR version (aka the '120 Trail') marketed straight after, which was a far more convincing scrambler, with knobby tyres and a high-mount front mudguard.

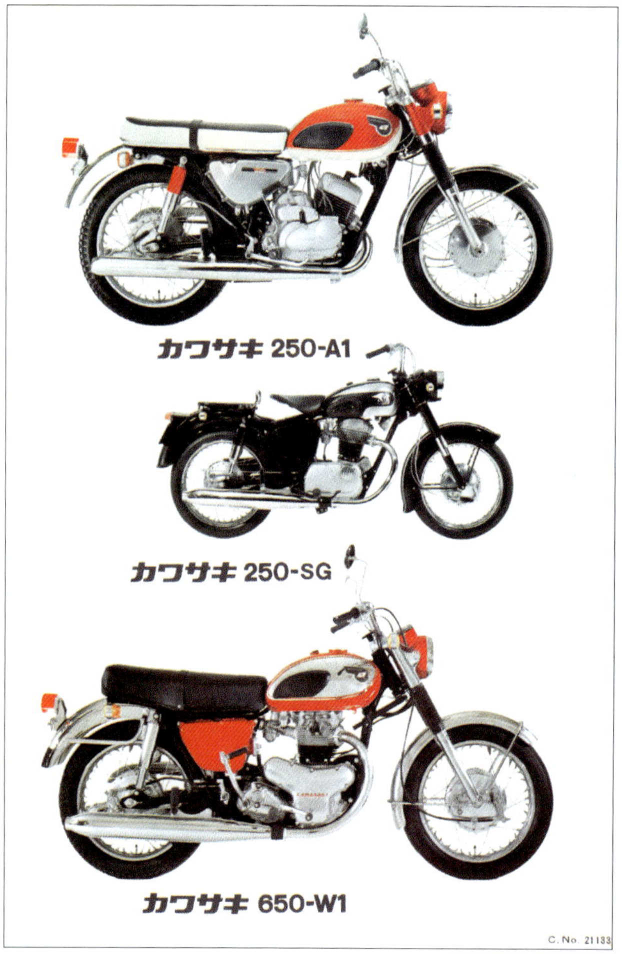

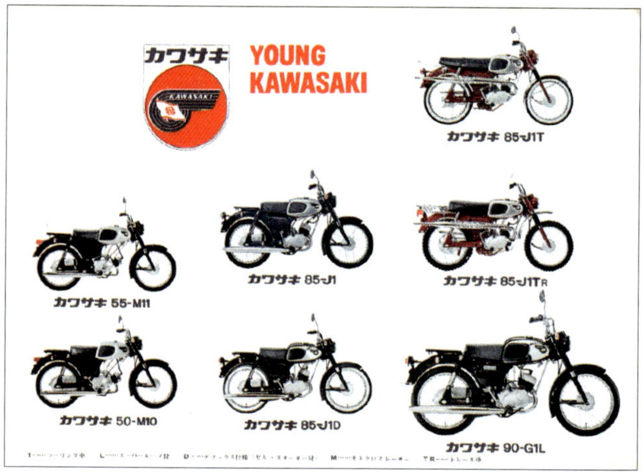

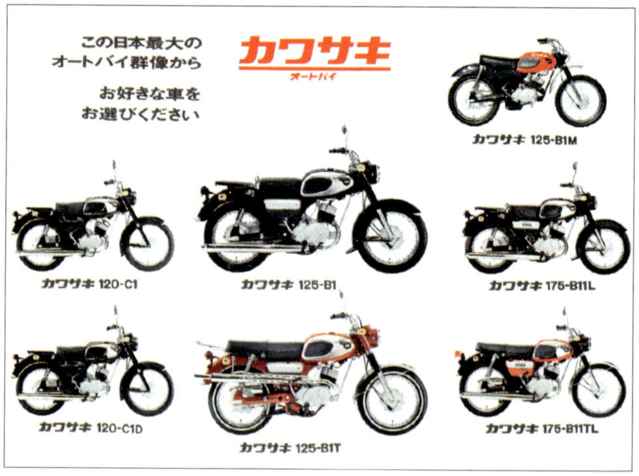

RIGHT The A7 'Avenger,' which was a huge success in America.

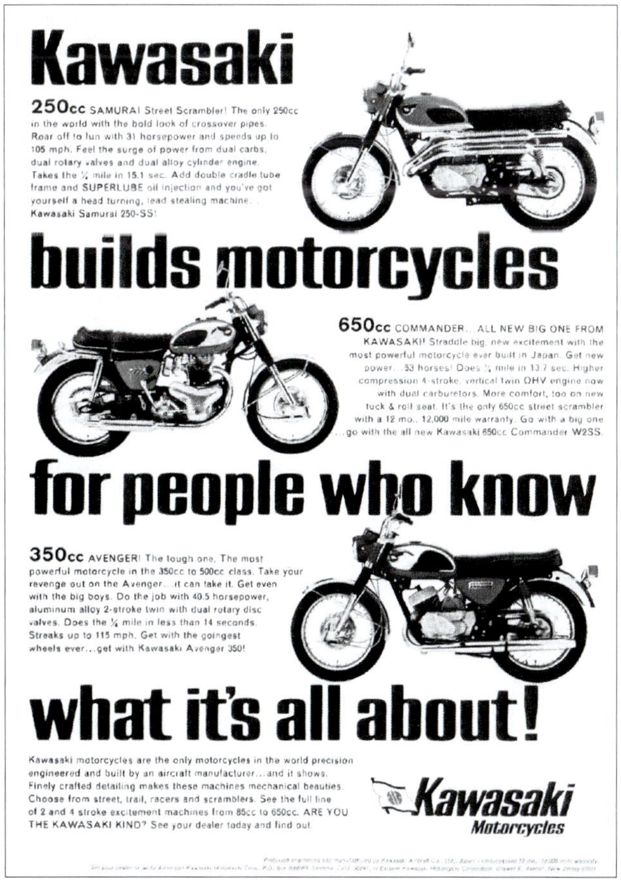

BELOW RIGHT American advertising from the summer of 1967, showing the W2SS with the best-selling 'Samurai' and 'Avenger' machines. Kawasaki listed around 30 model grades for the US market that year.

This 115cc machine was brought out alongside the 250 A1SS, which carried on the 'street scrambler' theme via a pair of pipes rising up from the engine to run beneath the seat line on the nearside. This was the perfect machine for American tastes and fashion trends at the time, with the model using the Samurai SS name in the States.

Another newcomer announced in February 1967 was the 350 A7. This 338cc model, known as the Avenger in North America, featured a bored-out version of the A1 engine, with a 62mm bore helping increase the power output to 40bhp. As it happens, a prototype 350 Avenger had been shown at the Disneyland Hotel in September 1966, displayed next to a 250 Samurai and the new A1-R racer that duly entered production at the end of that year. Most of the US advertising budget went on the 250 and 350 models, by the way, as these were the volume sellers for the Japanese marque. Indeed, once the A7 went on sale in April, demand for this $815 bike and the sporty SS grades far outstripped supply for several months.

The SS boom gave Kawasaki an ideal chance to relaunch the W1, using all the marketing techniques learnt over the previous few seasons, but backing up the gab via some fresh engineering as well, with twin-carburettors being the main new feature. As it happens, there had actually been a twin-carb version of the K, displayed as a prototype at the Tokyo Motor Show in Meguro days. Naturally, the idea wasn't wasted on the Kawasaki guys, and indeed a more powerful version of the W had been on the cards from the early stages of development. Sorting out the niggling post-launch problems delayed things a touch, though, and enthusiasts had to wait until the W2SS 'Commander' model entered production in April 1967 before they could get their hands on something with a little more punch. Even then, the 53bhp W2SS was only ever built for export, so domestic buyers would have to wait even longer.

Looking at the technical changes, with the W1 employing a cylinder head with an integrated intake

LEFT Close-up of the W2SS engine and transmission.

BOTTOM The W2SS flyer produced to announce the new twin-carb version of the W1 model, which was still available to special order in the States until 1968. Note the obligatory chequered flag badge on the oil tank, which was also applied to the box on the other side of the bike.

manifold, a new alloy head had to be produced to take the pair of carburettors (two VM28s instead of a single VM31 unit, each having a separate air filter), although the ten external cooling fins were carried over. Inside, the exhaust valves were the same diameter as before, but the inlets were a fraction larger, while a higher 9.0:1 c/r led to a modified block being adopted. There was a new oil tank, with fresh internals and the filler moved forward, closer to the engine, and a brand new exhaust system featuring Cabton-style mufflers on either side of the bike. These shorter exhaust pipes delivered quite a different sound to the original W1 setup, but whichever sounded the best was down to personal preference. There was no doubt that the SS sounded more sporting, and that was ultimately the aim of the designers, acting on requests from the various US dealerships. On saying that, the retention of mild camshaft timing meant the bike was still a smooth cruiser rather than a cafe racer in character. Rounding off the changes, the four-speed transmission was modified to make gear selections more positive. While the gearing was subtly different, the mechanism improvements were duly introduced on the strict W1 as well, making life easier for all Kawasaki 650 users, regardless of their level of mechanical sympathy.

Interestingly, the gauge of the metal was beefed-up on certain components to prevent vibration cracking, and this area of modification was also carried over to the W1. Unique to the W2SS, however, which sold for $1295 in America ($80 cheaper than the similar-spec BSA Lightning), was a newly-designed pleated seat, shorter mudguards front and rear covering a fresh wheel and tyre combination (as well as different tread patterns, there was a larger diameter wheel up front, and fatter rubber at both ends), and racy badges on the oil tank and side box.

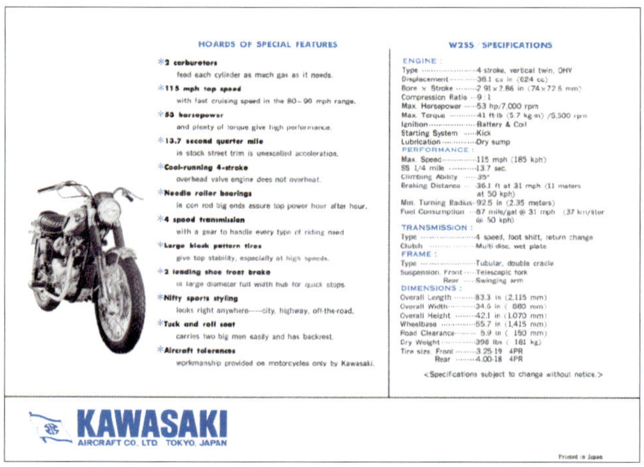

BELOW AND RIGHT Nearside and front three-quarter views of the W2SS. One can see the same badge was used on both sides of the machine. By the way, this is an early model, as all those sent to America had a pair of side reflectors built into the rear lamp unit in order to comply with the latest Federal regulations due to take effect on the first day of 1968.

BOTTOM Part of a brochure showing the A7SS and strict A7 for the US market.

BELOW LEFT The 650 W1SS, announced in the final days of 1967. Those without intimate knowledge of the Kawasaki marque would be hard pressed to tell the difference between this model and the W2SS, although the back of the engine gives a perfect identifying feature, as the W1SS has only a single carburettor rather than two. Note the reflector on the side of the rear light unit.

OPPOSITE, BOTTOM Catalogue for the W1P. Note the police bikes gained the SS-style oil filler arrangement after the latter's introduction.

BELOW RIGHT Detail shot of the red rear reflector fitted to the W-series, as required by US law for 1968. Corresponding amber-coloured front reflectors were usually added under the fuel tank, just inside the frame.

OPPOSITE, TOP & MIDDLE Brochure for the 1968 Model Year 53bhp W2SS and the 50bhp W1SS sister model. The specification table has been separated for ease of reference.

Kawasaki was on a roll now, with numerous AMA speed records claimed on the Bonneville Salt Flats (including one for the W1 thanks to Roger Hall), and having at last found the magic formula for volume sales. Following hot on the heels of a new modern-looking M50 moped came the G1TRL (a trail version of the 90cc G1 model), and then the 350 A7SS, or Avenger SS as it was known in America. This followed the familiar format set by the A1SS, and then, in December 1967, production of the 650 W1SS began.

Like the W2SS, the W1SS was built for export only, and featured the same short exhaust system and other modifications as the twin-carb model announced eight months earlier, but the old 50bhp engine. In reality, that about sums things up! Slightly cheaper than the W2SS, it gave Kawasaki three W models, albeit briefly, as the strict W1 was soon to fall by the wayside following the introduction of the W1 Special back in Japan.

W-series data register

Although it seemed unlikely at first, checking the details of a number of bikes for sale in Japan has provided the evidence to back up the suggestion in parts books and other official paperwork that all W-series used the same frame and engine serial number batch. Therefore, the frame numbers begin with W1F-00001, while the engine numbers run from W1E-00001 onwards.

THE W1 SPECIAL

Sitting alongside a W2SS reference model, the 53bhp W1 Special (or W1S) was displayed as a prototype at the 1967 Tokyo Show, which ran from October 27 to November 8 that year. For the record, only Honda, Suzuki, Kawasaki, Yamaha and Rabbit (Fuji) had bikes on display, and Rabbit would fail to turn up for the 1968 event. Nonetheless, interest in motorcycles was still high, with the remaining 'big four' fighting tooth and nail to garner sales, using a combination of glamour and new technology to reel in customers.

With domestic sales officially beginning in February 1968 (the W1S was not sold abroad), for a little while, the W1S was something of an oddity. While the twin-carb engine and four-speed transmission (albeit with slightly different gearing) was the same as that employed in the W2SS, the

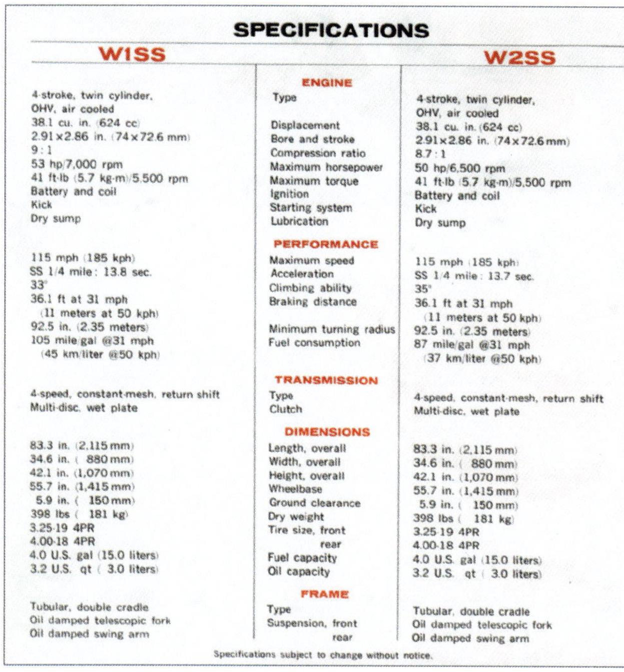

SPECIFICATIONS

W1SS		W2SS
	ENGINE	
4-stroke, twin cylinder, OHV, air cooled	Type	4-stroke, twin cylinder, OHV, air cooled
38.1 cu. in. (624 cc)	Displacement	38.1 cu. in. (624 cc)
2.91×2.86 in. (74×72.6 mm)	Bore and stroke	2.91×2.86 in. (74×72.6 mm)
9 : 1	Compression ratio	8.7 : 1
53 hp/7,000 rpm	Maximum horsepower	50 hp/6,500 rpm
41 ft-lb (5.7 kg-m)/5,500 rpm	Maximum torque	41 ft-lb (5.7 kg-m)/5,500 rpm
Battery and coil	Ignition	Battery and coil
Kick	Starting system	Kick
Dry sump	Lubrication	Dry sump
	PERFORMANCE	
115 mph (185 kph)	Maximum speed	115 mph (185 kph)
SS 1/4 mile: 13.8 sec.	Acceleration	SS 1/4 mile: 13.7 sec.
33°	Climbing ability	35°
36.1 ft at 31 mph (11 meters at 50 kph)	Braking distance	36.1 ft at 31 mph (11 meters at 50 kph)
92.5 in. (2.35 meters)	Minimum turning radius	92.5 in. (2.35 meters)
105 mile/gal @31 mph (45 km/liter @50 kph)	Fuel consumption	87 mile/gal @31 mph (37 km/liter @50 kph)
	TRANSMISSION	
4-speed, constant-mesh, return shift	Type	4-speed, constant-mesh, return shift
Multi-disc, wet plate	Clutch	Multi-disc, wet plate
	DIMENSIONS	
83.3 in. (2,115 mm)	Length, overall	83.3 in. (2,115 mm)
34.6 in. (880 mm)	Width, overall	34.6 in. (880 mm)
42.1 in. (1,070 mm)	Height, overall	42.1 in. (1,070 mm)
55.7 in. (1,415 mm)	Wheelbase	55.7 in. (1,415 mm)
5.9 in. (150 mm)	Ground clearance	5.9 in. (150 mm)
398 lbs (181 kg)	Dry weight	398 lbs (181 kg)
3.25-19 4PR	Tire size, front	3.25-19 4PR
4.00-18 4PR	rear	4.00-18 4PR
4.0 U.S. gal (15.0 liters)	Fuel capacity	4.0 U.S. gal (15.0 liters)
3.2 U.S. qt (3.0 liters)	Oil capacity	3.2 U.S. qt (3.0 liters)
	FRAME	
Tubular, double cradle	Type	Tubular, double cradle
Oil damped telescopic fork	Suspension, front	Oil damped telescopic fork
Oil damped swing arm	rear	Oil damped swing arm

Specifications subject to change without notice.

BELOW & BOTTOM Following on from the police bike theme, a fascinating W1 variant produced to special order for an Australian government body, featuring the regular W1 engine and exhaust system, but a number of SS features as well. Obviously destined for escort and parade duty, several were built, looking at the photos available. Interestingly, the Imperial family had bought a number of Harley 748s in early 1965. If they'd have waited just a little longer ...

BELOW Japanese advertising from the autumn of 1967, with the strict W1 still lining up alongside the A1 and A7, plus one of the tiddlers that were so popular amongst younger riders. There was a new W1 on display as a taster of things to come for home market enthusiasts at the 1967 Tokyo Show, by the way.

muffler on the sporting Cabton-type exhaust system was longer than that fitted to the contemporary SS export grades. The gauges were separated from the headlight, with a round speedometer placed next to a similar-looking tachometer, while the front indicators, although of the same design as before, were moved lower down; the rear indicators were unchanged, as was the rear light unit. The two-tone seat was easy to spot, while the mudguards were standard W1 fare (and as such, longer than those found on the SS models). Finishing touches included a modified steering damper, and the filler on the oil tank followed the SS pattern. Interestingly, the distinctive shield-shaped badge was only ever fitted to the nearside box.

For the record, although only eight of the original W1s were built in 1968, the strict W1 was still being listed as available until the start of 1969, priced at 328,000 yen, against 338,000 yen for the newcomer; this compared with just 268,000 yen for both the Honda CB450 and Suzuki T500. As such, the W1S became the only four-stroke Kawasaki sold in Japan once the 47bhp W1 disappeared, as

BELOW LEFT A 1968 W1 with a two-tone seat, and an A-series bike beyond it in the site 24 building. This type of seat was duly used on the first W1 Specials.

BOTTOM LEFT A Japanese advert from the June 1968 issue of *Autoby*, announcing the arrival of the new W1 Special. Note the early-type indicators, initially carried over from the strict W1 that this model effectively replaced.

plans to market the W2TT at home (one was displayed at the 1968 Tokyo Motor Show with the latest paintwork, but failed to arrive in dealerships, although dealers were allowed

BELOW RIGHT The W1 Special, or W1S, at the time of its announcement.

BOTTOM RIGHT The W2P, which was renamed the W1SP after the W1 Special was given a minor face-lift at the tail-end of 1968.

to order the TT's special exhaust system for customers who wanted it) were thwarted after the bike received a lukewarm response in Tokyo.

In many ways, one can be forgiven for thinking the original W1S was conceived as a way to use up old components left in the parts bin, for the W1 Special had only been on sale a few months, when it was promptly given a number of cosmetic revisions. Going on sale in the autumn of 1968, the updated W1S featured an SS-style black pleated seat, the shorter SS pattern mudguards, new bullet-shaped indicators front and rear, and new gauges with fresh graphics, a clearer red line marking and added a tripometer.

In the meantime, the company was still busy introducing smaller models, such as the 169cc F3 and F2, and the 89cc 90S GA1 and 90SS GA2. In addition, more improvements were made to the assembly lines during March 1968, along with the opening of a new building purely for pilot builds to improve production techniques before a bike was launched. A few months later, a long test straight was completed inside the Akashi factory complex; still there to this day.

会社案内
川崎航空機工業株式会社

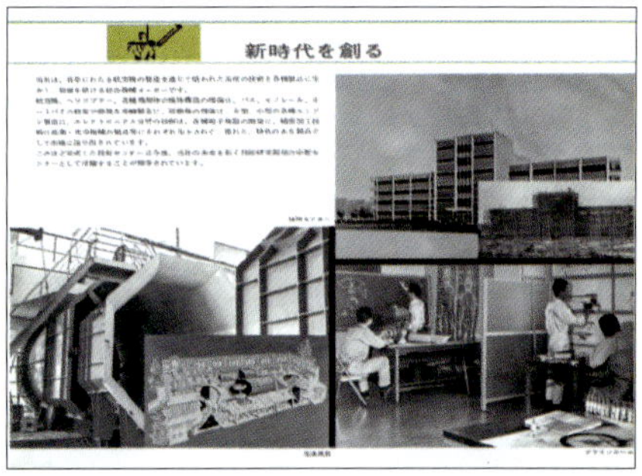
新時代を創る

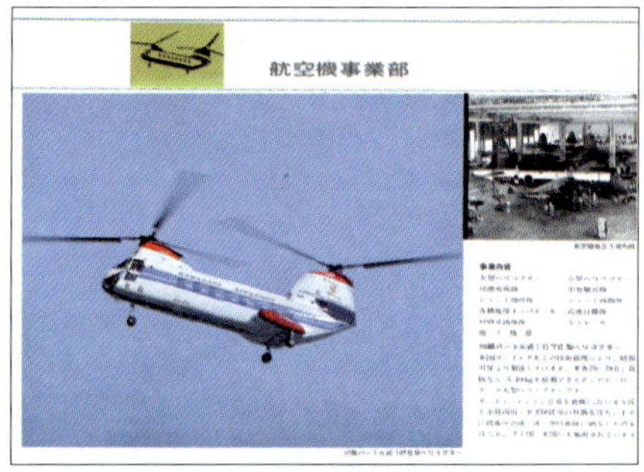
航空機事業部

単車事業部

発動機事業部

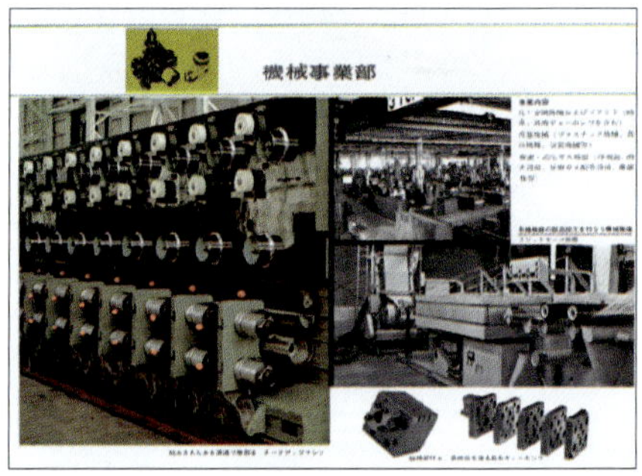
機械事業部

自動車事業部

ジェットエンジン工場

産業と文化の繁栄に奉仕する……
……川崎グループ

OPPOSITE Superb brochure from the spring of 1968 showing the scope of Kawasaki's incredibly varied industrial activities under the KAC banner. In addition to those illustrated here, taking in design, aircraft, motorcycles, commercial engines (including two- and four-stroke petrol units, plus diesel engines), machinery (soon to include early industrial robots), buses, and jet engines (production and overhaul), it also had pages covering training and education, as well as leisure and welfare. The back page is fascinating, too, with pictures of the bullet train, ships, shipping and steel manufacturing being chosen to represent other arms of the Kawasaki empire, although most would ultimately be brought back together after the KHI reshuffle in 1969.

BELOW One of the last Japanese dealer adverts placed before the W1S face-lift.

BELOW LEFT Various views of the domestic market W1 Special (or W1S) as it looked at the end of 1968, following a mild face-lift. The W1S was only ever made available in red or blue.

Next up was the W2TT, which had been rumoured for some time, but didn't enter production until May 1968. This was basically nothing more than a W2SS with an upswept exhaust, with both pipes mounted high up on the nearside, and separate instruments like those found on the W1S to allow wannabe racers to remove the headlight; it was also easy to ditch the mufflers for those serious about their sport. The model's unique '650TT' badge (although 650ST would have been more sensible, as the 'sports touring' moniker was applied to this particular variant) was fitted to the box on the nearside only, and while there were plans to market the TT in Japan, it was destined to remain purely for export.

If the shelf life of the original W1S was brief, that of the first generation W2TT was fated to be even shorter. This is because Kawasaki decided to display the 1969 model at the 1968 Tokyo Show in October, which featured a completely different fuel tank (designed by 'Molly,' as it happens) and exhaust system, as well as a silver-coloured sidebox and oil tank, and a blacked out area around the black-painted headlight casing. While the TT would not go on sale in Japan, the seed had been sown, and American enthusiasts knew exactly what to expect in the coming weeks. With the W1 dropping from US price lists, the 1969 W2SS and W1SS would also adopt these latest cosmetic upgrades, plus the W1 Special exhaust system, giving the W-series an altogether more modern look.

THIS PAGE Catalogue for the W1S dating from late 1968, showing the model on the production lines and an aerial view of the Akashi works. There were also some pictures of police bikes included, but these were actually K-series models, so have been left out here.

OPPOSITE, LEFT Atmospheric shot of someone having fun with an A1SS on the test course which officially opened at the end of 1968. Workers in the buildings to either side were often treated to the sound of racing machines on full tilt, as well as regular production machines. The concrete bumps were naturally placed with the latter in mind, in order to test suspensions.

OPPOSITE, RIGHT Promotional paperwork for the 90SS.

On the subject of the 1968 Tokyo Show, the launch of the Honda CB750 seemed to overshadow everything, and news of it leaking beforehand led Kawasaki to cancel any thoughts of displaying its 750cc four-cylinder prototype at the event, codenamed N600. Rumours of an 800cc twin were also being banded about, more likely to take attention away from the N600 project, which was still a well-kept secret. There were also mutterings within the industry about a two-stroke triple, and that mystery machine would evolve into a showroom model. But not yet. Even though it entered pilot production in September, the triple was not exhibited in Tokyo, prompting one writer to say "Kawasaki has nothing new to display," in his show report. This comment was from a Japan point of view, of course, but there were no complaints from Paris, where Kawasaki had a full line display at the 1968 Paris Salon courtesy of its new distributor in France. Anyway, with Christmas 1968 out of the way, things were set to get very exciting indeed ...

W-series timeline

A summary of major W-series developments, putting things into chronological order. For leading specifications and production numbers, please refer to Appendix I.

- October 1965 – prototype W1 displayed at the 12th Tokyo Show.
- March 1966 – the 50bhp W1 officially goes on sale in America, priced at $1195. Production for the domestic market begins at the same time, Japan's 47bhp 650 W1 ultimately listed at 328,000 yen.
- July 1966 – release of W1P for police work.
- April 1967 – release of twin-carb 53bhp W2SS 'Commander' for export only. SS stands for 'street scrambler,' although there was very little resemblance to a motocross machine! As such, 'street sports' is probably closer to reality.
- December 1967 – release of W1SS 'Commander' for export only. This was a single-carb version of the W2SS, inheriting the shorter Cabton-style exhaust and chassis upgrades found on that model.
- February 1968 – release of 338,000 yen 650 W1S (or 650 W1 'Special'), which was basically the domestic version of the W2SS. The W2P police bike is launched at the same time, which was later renamed the W1SP.
- May 1968 – release of W2TT for export only. This was basically a W2SS with a raised exhaust system, and a detachable headlight. Although 'sports touring' has been put forward in official paperwork, TT more likely stands for 'trail and touring'.
- February 1971 – release of 53bhp 650 W1SA, mainly for the home market. Priced at 348,000 yen and built until December 1972, it was the first W model with a 'left shift, right brake' arrangement. The W1SAP police bike is announced at the same time.
- September 1972 – production of the 53bhp W3 (or 650-RS) begins with disc brakes and numerous anti-pollution measures. While production ended in December 1973, this final W variant (initially priced at 363,000 yen) was sold from February 1973 until the early part of the 1976 season.
- 1977 MY – indirectly replaced by the Z650 (KZ650-B1).

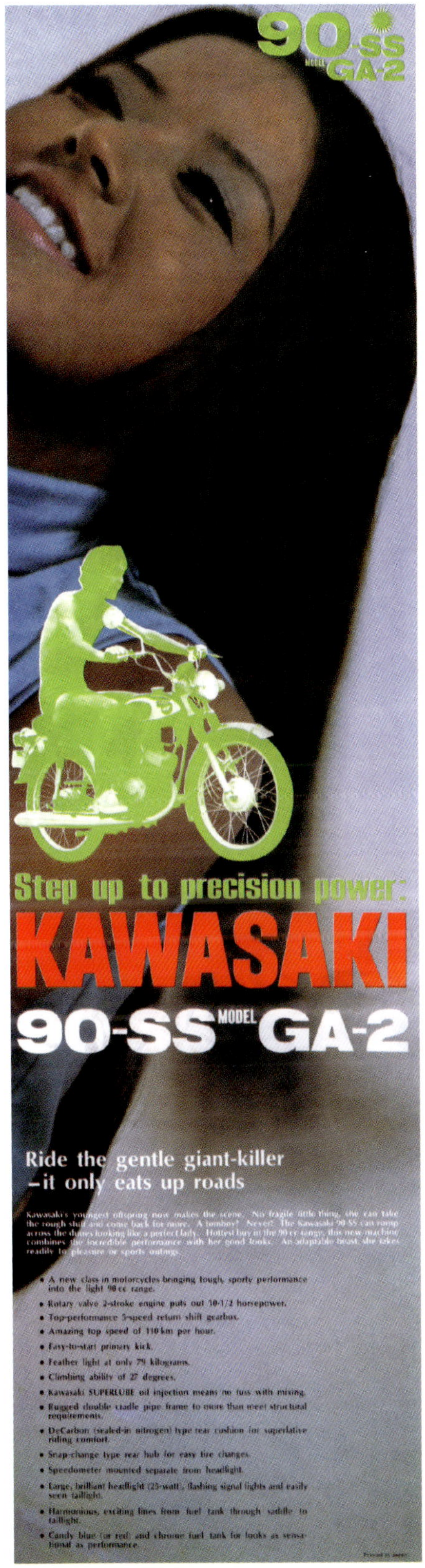

LEFT A good selection of W1S and A-series models being loaded up for delivery to home market distributors.

BELOW LEFT Different views to those seen in the catalogue of the early, somewhat shortlived W2TT.

BELOW RIGHT Catalogue for the original W2TT.

BELOW AND RIGHT American catalogue for the 1969 Model Year W2TT and W2SS.

BOTTOM Japanese advertising from the end of 1968. Something very special would soon be swelling the ranks at Kawasaki …

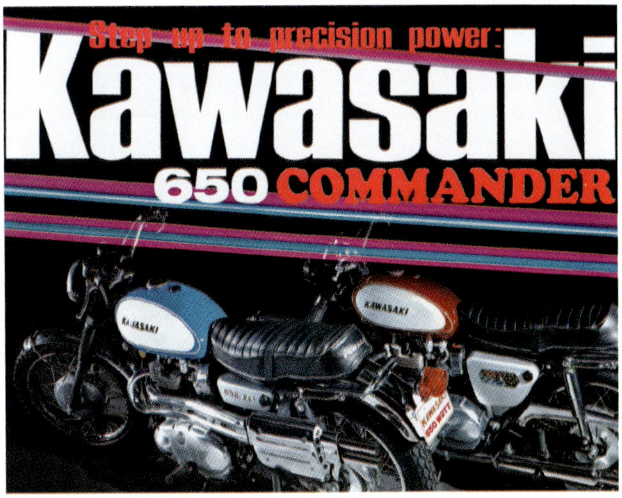

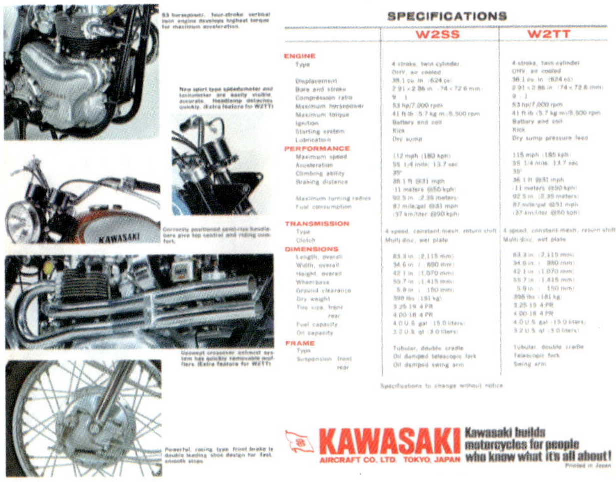

3 THE H1 & H2 MODELS

While survival was still far from guaranteed in a fickle industry led as much by fashion trends as depth of engineering, the W-series had hurled the Kawasaki motorcycle brand onto the world stage in no uncertain terms. Kawasaki's next masterpiece – using two- rather than four-stroke technology – was intended to be a statement that the Akashi company could roll with the best in the business. And what a convincing statement it was. It served as a warning to others that after so many years of being a minor player, Kawasaki was now fully committed to two-wheelers and here to stay ...

LEFT & OPPOSITE TOP Catalogue for the 338,000 yen W1 Special (or W1S) featuring images from a meeting for W owners.

The W-series was the only four-stroke model left in the Kawasaki line-up by this time. It was a nice bike, sure enough, but it was hardly a ball of fire, and larger displacement machines were being developed left, right and centre by the competition, leaving it further in the shade in the speed stakes. The 350cc A7 'Avenger' was quick enough for most people, but it's amazing how much kudos is attached to barroom bragging rights – the glamour of horsepower and speed was always a draw amongst motorcycle enthusiasts, and still is to this day, even though buyers can only ever use a fraction of a superbike's performance in the real world. The dark art of marketing is a wonderful tool, tapping into areas of the mind that can't resist things that we know are far from sensible, convincing us that we need that little bit of excess in our lives in order to sleep at night. Enter the Kawasaki Mach III, and the finishing touches in the creation of Kawasaki's sporting image – an image that was further nurtured via new lines of high-performance machines over the decades to come.

BOTTOM LEFT The A7SS in home market guise.

BELOW MIDDLE & RIGHT The 1969 Model Year version of the W2TT, with a different exhaust system and a number of cosmetic upgrades. The so-called MY changes (introduced in autumn 1968 for 1969 in this case) were increasingly used as part of a co-ordinated marketing plan in the States, although this particular model, like the W1SS, was destined to last for less than one sales season, however. Indeed, the 1969 W1SS must be the rarest of all Kawasakis.

LEFT The W2SS received the same face-lift as the W2TT for 1969, as did a handful of bikes from the W1SS line. With the W1 Special (W1S) having been revised at home as well, and no more strict W1 models being built, the entire W-series was now modernized and ready to move forward into the 1969 season.

BELOW Osamu Tanegashima was instrumental in helping get the US side of the business turned around, as well as one of the key instigators in the N100 project. After being attached to the export department, he was later involved in the development of the Z1.

KAWASAKI'S ROAD ROCKET

The autumn of 1968 saw the 90 G3SS, G3TR and GA3/90SSS tiddlers enter production, along with the highly-successful 250 F4 scrambler, but it was the 125mph (200kph) H1 air-cooled triple that's the important model as far as we're concerned, given the scope of this book.

The first pre-production machine was sent to America to be exhibited at a dealer event in Washington's Hilton Hotel in September 1968. Oddly, though, the H1 (or KH500A) was not displayed at that year's Tokyo Show, despite the bike's obvious technical appeal. After all, this was the world's first volume-produced two-stroke vertical triple (the earlier DKW triple was a racer, the Olympus SH prototype made by Katayama Sangyo was hardly mass-production, and the contemporary Triumph Trident and BSA Rocket were four-stroke machines), but Kawasaki was probably right in letting Honda take the glory with its CB750 – a motorcycle that commanded more column inches than probably any Japanese machine before it, and it was folly to try and

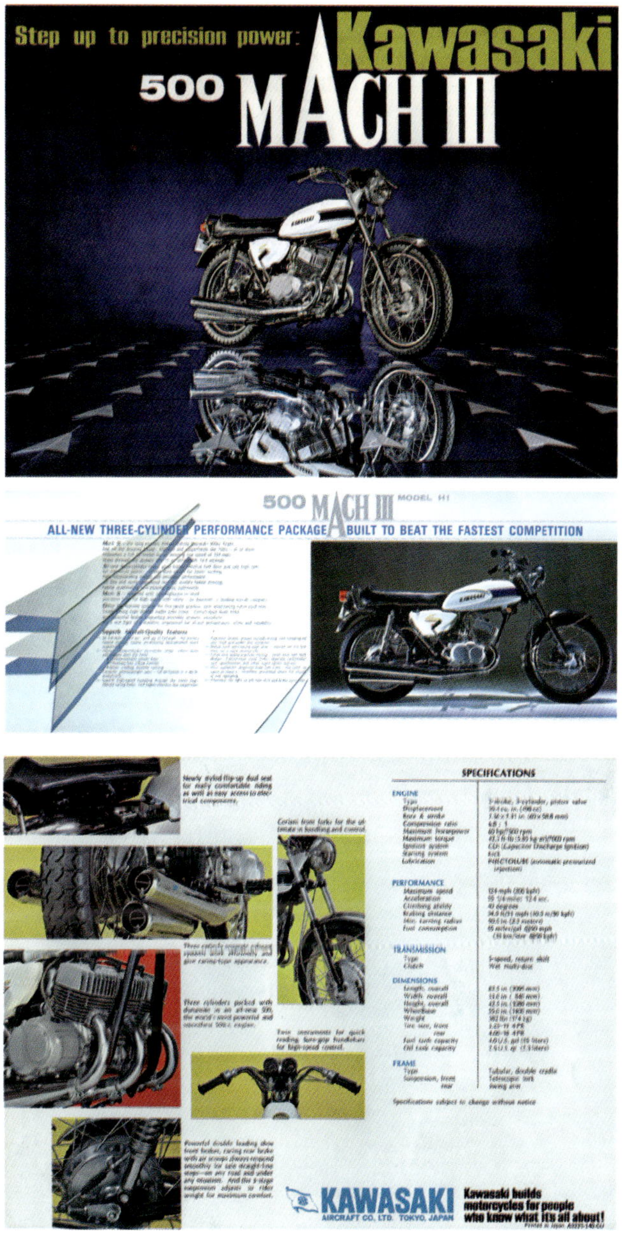

RIGHT First catalogue for the Mach III.

compete with Honda's PR push, especially as the bike was only destined to be sold abroad initially. This debut also killed off the N600 project, as we mentioned in the last chapter, although it did raise the bar for the Z1, but more on that later ...

Once the post-show dust settled, people's attention soon switched to Kawasaki's new 500cc three-cylinder model, as anticipated, for US sales began in January 1969 after an extensive Stateside test session conducted three months earlier. Competing directly with Suzuki's T500, introduced in 1968 at $1039, the H1 was named the '500 Mach III' in America, and the press went wild. *Cycle World* wrote that the new bike would "raise the hairs on the back of a rider's neck, or turn them grey in 13 seconds flat. At top speed, it will run faster than the Osaka Express. It will trounce any mass production motorcycle that comes in full street trim, regardless of displacement. The stench of rubber smoke and a 100ft long black strip give ample evidence that it has departed, yet it is as docile as a kitten. Its POE price of $999 is incredibly low, but it puts out more honest-to-goodness horsepower than a Manx Norton."

Initial development of the H1 had started in May 1967, based on a bold request from Kawasaki's men in America, using the N100 project code. The main points listed by the US team were a sub-13 second standing-quarter time, a top speed of over 125mph (200kph), a low price point, preferably under $1000, and dynamic styling unlike anything to come from Japan beforehand. Reliability was taken as read, of course.

After the initial shock of being asked for something only previously feasible in racing machinery, Hiroyuki Matsumoto began working on the engine specs in Akashi. Once it was ascertained that the cooling of the central cylinder in the line of three was not compromised (a series of wind tunnel tests using a modified A1 were conducted early on, in July 1967, to make absolutely sure), the decision to go with an air-cooled triple was easy to justify, as, compared to a twin of the same displacement (the other option on the table until quite a late stage in the design process), the extra pot allowed smoother running and smaller power pulses for each cylinder, which in turn allowed a lighter clutch and transmission to be used. In addition, the third cylinder gave a greater port area, thus increasing the potential of releasing more horsepower per litre (in order to reach the target speed requested, it was calculated that a minimum of 58bhp would be needed to overcome wind resistance), and smaller bores would also enhance combustion at higher rpm

BOTTOM LEFT AND RIGHT A couple of views of the three-cylinder styling mock-up, again executed using clay. The forks are taking shape, although the final versions would be made in steel rather than the aluminum alloy used by Ceriani, and the trendy fender stripe was ultimately left off. Production bikes had a frame a little longer than this one in order to calm down the handling, which was a tad sharp with the shorter wheelbase.

BELOW A clay mock-up for the N100 project, this one featuring a twin-cylinder engine. Development continued with two- and three-pot units until engineers were able to confirm sufficient cooling efficiency for the central cylinder.

given the traditional piston-valve arrangement employed. In effect, Kawasaki would gain a high-revving unit not that much bigger or heavier than a regular half-litre twin, whilst picking up a ton of Brownie points for technical innovation.

With the advantage of being able to design the triple from scratch – virtually every part was unique to the H1 – the engineering team was able to choose a bore/stroke relationship that best served its purpose rather than being hindered by having certain areas dictated by standardization considerations. As such, once the N100 project was given a rubber stamp, a 60mm bore and 58.8mm stroke was specified, giving the all-alloy unit a cubic capacity of 498cc.

The two-piece diecast aluminium alloy crankcase was split horizontally through the crankshaft centerline, while the multi-section crank itself ran in six main bearings, each being a ball bearing strategically sized to reduce heat generation. The engine employed remarkably short connecting rods in order to keep overall unit dimensions as compact as possible, with needle bearings at the big-ends, while the pistons (which ran in cast-iron cylinder liners) were secured using gudgeon pins. Lubrication was via a

positive-feed 'Injectolube' oil injection system linked to the throttle. On the subject of throttles, three Mikuni VM28SC carbs were specified, with a single large air filter attached. With a 6.8:1 compression ratio, the three-cylinder unit pulled strongly at 6000rpm, with a peak of 60bhp listed at 7500rpm, although there was still 40bhp available at 9000rpm.

BELOW Cutaway drawing of the H1/Mach III engine. A five-port piston-valve system was used after other induction systems proved unsuitable on the compact three-cylinder layout, made only a touch wider by the AC generator and ignition distributor at either side. This drawing also highlights the cooling fin designs, which are tight to the cylinder on the inboard side of the outer pots, allowing the central cylinder more fin area.

BOTTOM Power was a key development point for the Kawasaki engineering team – to produce the fastest, most powerful bike available. Backing up the brawn, the triple exhaust layout was an impressive sight, and made an impressive sound, too; each pipe was separate on the early models.

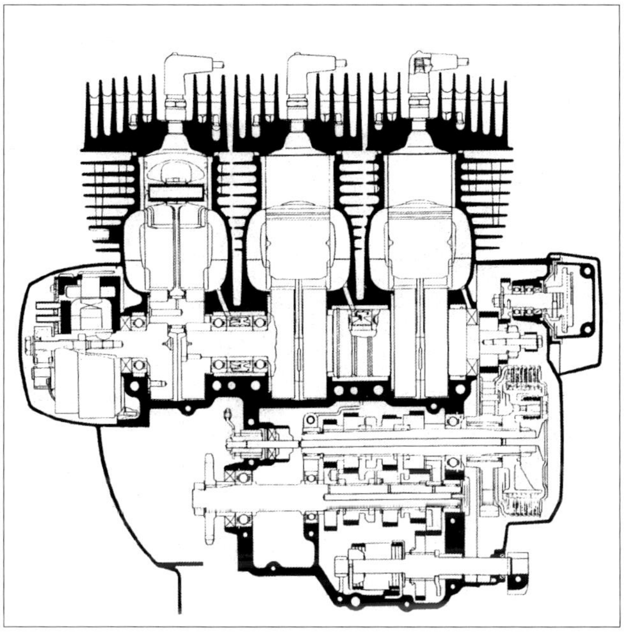

After abandoning the idea of four pipes for aesthetic balance, the H1 delivered a very distinctive exhaust note from the three asymmetrically set mufflers (two on one side, one on the other), sounding just like a racing machine once one got a few thousand revs on the clock. The high-revving powerplant was a delight for users, of course, but a real headache for the engineering team, led by Yukio Otsuki. Michiharu Tsukamoto had asked Otsuki to join the motorcycle division in 1962, duly moving on the racing side. After taking a year out on a research mission with a German gas turbine specialist, Otsuki duly returned to the department, and from 1968, held the position of motorcycle engine design chief.

Anyway, at that time, a traditional ignition with points (or contact breakers) would not have been able to handle engine speeds in the 10,000rpm sphere, so electronic ignition was investigated, ultimately leading to the use of a capacitive discharge (CDI) system. Even then, to keep service schedules sensible, sparkplug technology had to be refined to suit the 25,000 volts delivered by the CDI setup, and Kawasaki's engineers eventually opted for surface gap plugs, often used in outboard engines. There was an added bonus, for as well as having a longer life than regular sparkplugs (up to four times longer according to contemporary adverts), the gap remained constant, and, combined with the CDI's high voltage, it delivered a stronger spark over a wider area, reducing fouling whilst improving combustion and fuel efficiency.

BELOW American advertising for the Mitsubishi-designed CDI system.

BOTTOM RIGHT Production version of the Mach III with US lighting.

OPPOSITE The Mach III was sold in Europe long before it was made available in Japan. Note the front and rear indicators, not fitted on US models, and the lack of side markers under the fuel tank. The rear mudguard was also a touch longer on most but not all of the European bikes, adding 10mm (0.4in) to the overall length when fitted, and there was generally a choice of handlebar profiles, too.

For Europe, though, sourcing the special Champion plugs was not always easy, and a new three-coil system hooked up to a unique distributor with three points was devised, allowing regular NGKs to be used. This ignition setup was duly employed in the USA and Japan as well, albeit a little later. For the record, according to the parts book, bikes sporting CDI carried the KA-1 designation, while the three-coil, three-point distributor versions carried a KA-2 one.

The engine sat leaning forward in a double-loop tubular steel frame, following its profile at the leading edge; rubber mounts were tried at one point, but ultimately found to be unnecessary. The five-speed transmission used unit construction, employing the rearmost part of the upper and lower crankcase castings to house the gearset. It gave the bike a neat appearance, with the 'bottom neutral' shift on the nearside, or left-hand side if you're the rider. Drive went through a multi-plate clutch before a nearside-mounted chain transferred it to the rear wheel, with the clutch lever on the left-hand side of the handlebars.

The frame, overseen by Toshio Togashi and Kunishige Onoda, was compared to that of a certain racing Norton by some, but most simply praised its rigidity, which allowed the suspension to work properly. Newly-designed, Ceriani-inspired telescopic front forks were specified up front, being particularly slim in order to get as much cooling air to the engine as possible, and attached to a hydraulic steering damper, while the rear-end used a conventional swing-arm arrangement with the three-step chrome shocks sporting exposed springs. Stainless steel mudguards were used at both ends, covering 3.25-19 rubber at the front, and 4.00-18s at the back, with both tyres initially being Japanese Dunlop Gold Seal K77s made exclusively for the high-speed H1 model. Braking was via drums at both ends (with an air

scoop added at the back), with the front brake lever on the right, next to the throttle, and the rear brake pedal on the offside, just below the kickstart crank. Interestingly, one was able to swap over the shift and rear brake locations on the early machines, although whether anyone actually did this is another matter altogether.

As for cosmetics, the 12V electrical system included a chrome headlight mounted in a silver-painted area surrounding it, that also provided a place for the bullet-shaped indicators to sit (when fitted). Matching indicators were attached just underneath the trailing edge of the seat, with a rear lamp aft of them, slightly higher up, and sporting a single reflector at the top, along with one on each side, teaming up with a pair of front side markers underneath the fuel tank. There was a speedometer on the left and a tachometer on the right, both separate items sitting between the shapely handlebars. The US-designed fuel tank was long and narrow, painted white with dark blue graphics and 'Kawasaki' script, while the dual seat (which flipped up to allow access to the bike's electrical components) was black with white piping. A 'Mach III 500' metal badge was fitted on the white side box, while an 'Electronic Ignition' decal was applied on the oil tank, which was also white with the filler at its trailing edge.

Why Mach III? Well, the author had thought that maybe it was because Ford had the Mach I, and Bridgestone was selling a Mach II at the time, but later there would be a whole host of Mach models fielded by Kawasaki, so that theory doesn't work. I have seen a few people note that the III is to signify three cylinders, and this may be true, but again, that theory falls down, too, as the range expanded, although the III moniker sits perfectly within the line as it grows, so perhaps it was planned with this in mind from the start. The bottom line is, most people were having too much fun to care! The *Cycle World* article continued: "The Mach III, in spite of its racer-like tendencies, is far from being a beast. It starts easily, has terrific brakes, is extremely manageable in traffic, and forgives the rider if he lets the engine speed drop too low. One would never know that the 500 is a racer in disguise, were it not for the fact that the front wheel readily lifts into the air if the throttle is jerked on in the first three gears."

Let's leave the last words to *Cycle* magazine, following its run at the Yatabe test track: "[Kawasaki] has thrown together from the ground up one of the most devastating two-wheelers ever to happen on the scene."

LEFT & INSET Fascinating images of an alternative paint and trim scheme using a flower theme, probably for use as a show exhibit. It seems odd, seeing as the 'Flower Power' era had peaked, and most of the hippies were part of the anti-bike movement. It also flies in the face of the purity of the Mach III's lines and purpose. But history is history, and I am here to record, not question ...

BELOW Yoji Hamawaki (left) and Masashi Isano outside the new KMC office at 1062 McGaw Avenue. For the record, McGaw Ave was officially still part of Santa Ana at this time, as Irvine had yet to be recognized as a city. Note the 'Flying K' logo at the start of the Kawasaki name, newly created by graphic artist Nick Nichols for just $100. Used initially by KMC only, it was later adopted by Kawasaki as a global symbol for the company.

ANOTHER US RESHUFFLE

The last chapter saw Kawasaki's American arm finally taking shape, but it was the last day of 1968 that brought about the final stage in its metamorphosis, for this is the day that the AKM and EKM operations merged to form Kawasaki Motors Corporation USA, or KMC as it was usually known. With the Iwaki-Hamawaki pairing still in command, initially, the business stayed in Gardena (aka Japan Town), but by February 1969, new, much larger premises had been secured at 1062 McGaw Avenue in what is today's Irvine, CA, right next to the Route 55 freeway on the Santa Ana border. Based closer to regular American businesses, allowing the company to employ staff with a better feel for the US market, this property was huge compared to the old Gardena office, but still proved too small over the coming months. A new sales office was duly opened close by, looking after around 900 dealers by that time, as well as a second administration building housing the computer section, and a parts warehouse.

There was no doubt Kawasaki was on a roll, as the complexion of US motorcycling changed completely. 1968 calendar year (CY) imports totalled 225,262 bikes for the year in America – about 45,000 units down on the previous year, and, of that total, Japanese imports accounted for 162,271 units. Imports of UK machines were about half those of 1967 at 26,453 units, and Italy was in a similar position. American Kawasaki sales, meanwhile, amounted to around 20,000 units for 1968, which can be expressed as either a fair percentage of US market share or, put another

BELOW A stunning advert for the 1969 US line-up, with a new Mach III on the cover, and (from left to right), the A7, A1SS, A7SS, G3, A1, W2TT, W2SS, W1SS, F4 (placed in the centre), F21M, G3TR, F3, C2TR and C2SS.

BOTTOM LEFT & RIGHT The H1 making headlines in the States ...

BELOW American advertising appealing to the speed freak fraternity.

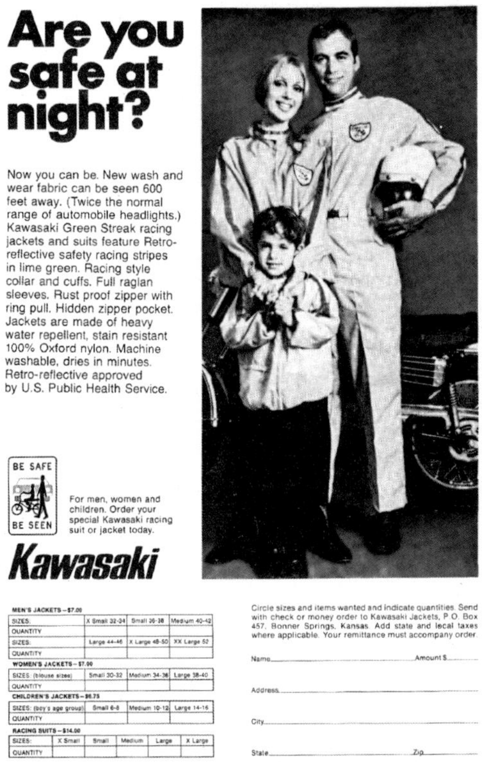

BELOW For the Kawasaki fan with everything – reflective 'Green Streak' racing jackets and suits in the company's signature lime green hue.

way, about the same amount of bikes moved as all of Italy's manufacturers put together for the year.

Anyway, the establishment of KMC allowed a more co-ordinated plan of attack on the marketing front, with things like Model Year changes introduced, and a more focused dealer network, working hand-in-hand with a central office. As it happens, with America being so big, a number of regional offices handling sales, spares and technical assistance were set up over the next few years to improve responsiveness, but Kawasaki was definitely moving in the right direction, becoming a truly professional outfit that realized keeping the dealers happy was the key to the company's own success. Having the right models at the right time was one way of ensuring a good relationship, and Kawasaki was suddenly blessed with a wealth of popular machines, with the flagship Mach III standing out as something very special. Indeed, despite a 'performance bike' boom in the USA, demand for the Mach III took everyone by surprise. No less than 4500 units were shipped to the States in the first half of 1969, but officials stated at the time that they could have moved twice as many as they received!

LEFT Kiyoshi Yotsumoto (left), Masashi Isano (centre) and Masao Ueda shaking hands on reaching an agreement on the KHI merger.

BELOW As well as the high-performance angle, Kawasaki was keen to start pushing its off-road credentials, too. In addition to doing extremely well in amateur racing in the States, Yamaha was dominating the lucrative scrambler market at this time – a situation that needed addressing.

KHI REBORN

There was very little in the way of new models released in early 1969 – a few tiddlers (the 90 GA0 and 100 G31M), plus a mini-bike called the Coyote. This is partly because the range had settled down, and partly because the factory was busy dealing with other things.

One will remember Kojiro Matsukata from the first chapter, and his dream of Kawasaki leading the way on land, on the sea and in the air. In reality, the dream never changed, and with zaibatsu no longer being a dirty word, Masashi Isano (the President of Kawasaki Heavy Industries, or what was the Kawasaki Dockyard Co. until the end of 1939) mooted the idea of bringing the major Kawasaki companies together to form an industrial giant with shared ideals and strong investor appeal. Similar mergers had taken place within Ishikawajima (or IHI) in 1960 and Mitsubishi four years later, so this was nothing unusual.

Isano's plans were drawn up in the spring of 1968, but even after Kiyoshi Yotsumoto (KAC's boss) and Masao Ueda (the President of Kawasaki Sharyo, or Kawasaki Rolling Stock Manufacturing Company) agreed to the merger, it took many months to hammer out the details and allow a smooth transition. Summing things up, the original Kawasaki Heavy Industries concern would be the main component in this new business, with KAC and the Rolling Stock enterprises effectively swallowed by it. Although there was a great deal of pride within each party, it ultimately made sense. The Kawasaki Heavy Industries (KHI) moniker was retained for this new firm, with Isano at the helm as its first President, and Yotsumoto and Ueda named as VPs; Kimiyo Nagano was given an honourary position as director and senior advisor.

The new KHI concern was divided into five main departments (shipbuilding, trains, aeronautical, machinery, plus engines and motorcycles), with three separate smaller divisions (ironwork, hydraulic machines, and Akashi Kikai, which was another machine maker, including robotics). Officially trading from April 1, 1969 and with a paid-in capital of a staggering 28,000,000,000 yen, this was the last major structural change to take place within the company until 2002. At the same time, Iseki made an investment to create the Iseki Kawasaki Service (IKS) sales company to handle general purpose engines for agricultural and other applications, thus completing the picture.

Meanwhile, motorcycle sales were taking off, and employment within the Kawasaki empire had slowly been rising as the sixties progressed as well, jumping from 17,205 in 1968 to over 30,000 by the end of 1969. This reflected the increase in capacity at Akashi, going up to a maximum of 15,000 units a month by the summer of 1969, thanks to additional machining, welding, spraying, plating and

H-series data register

A summary of H-series frame and engine start numbers, along with the main paint schemes used for each model according to Model Year release.

MY	Type	Frame No	Engine No	Colouring
1969	H1	KAF-00001 on	KAE-00001 on	Midnight White with blue.
1970	H1	KAF-06727 on	KAE-06315 on	Peacock Grey with black, Candy Red with white.
1971	H1A	KAF-23626 on	KAE-21876 on	Candy Blue with silver, Candy Red with white.
1972	H1B	KAF-48763 on	KAE-54101 on	Pearl Candy Orange with orange.
	H1C	KAF-48664 on	KAE-43902 on	Pearl Candy Orange with orange.
	H2	H2F-00001 on	H2E-00001 on	Pearl Candy Blue with blue, Candy Gold with red.
1973	H1D	H1F-00001 on	KAE-70024 on	Candy Lime with lime, Candy Green with lime.
	H2A	H2F-23671 on	H2E-23158 on	Candy Gold with orange, Candy Purple with orange.
1974	H1E	H1F-17001 on	KAE-87001 on	Candy Green with lime, Candy Red with red.
	H2B	H2F-32201 on	H2E-32401 on	Candy Brown with gold, Candy Green with lime.
1975	H1F	H1F-32400 on	KAE102400 on	Candy Sky Blue with blue, Candy Brown with gold.
	H2C	H2F-42547 on	H2E-42827 on	Candy Super Red with red, Candy Purple with purple.

packing facilities. Yet another packing area was created at a new site 60 building, which handled export crating, and the company started building snowmobile engines during this period, too, mainly for the North American market. By the time autumn came along, the site 14 shop had been completed, dedicated to fuel tank painting. It was an incredibly busy time at the factory, with rapid expansion on all fronts, taking Kawasaki's bike business out of the red for the first time in September 1969.

With Isano moving into the Chairman's office a few months after the reshuffle, Kiyoshi Yotsumoto duly became President of KHI in November 1969. It was a fascinating era, with new technology being promoted and used to the full, with 1970 at last seeing gas turbines on test in various vehicles, laying the foundation for Kawasaki's KG72 prototype (the company's first in-house developed gas turbine) of 1972.

THE 1969 TOKYO MOTOR SHOW

The Mach III was hardly new by the time the Tokyo Show came around, as America had had it from the beginning of the year, and Europe soon after that. But it was still big news for at last domestic sales had started, officially beginning on September 1, 1969. Other than the lighting, a ribbed front tyre to help improve the beast's handling characteristics, and a subtle gearing change that reduced the top speed by a fraction, the 500cc bike was the same as the model making waves in the States.

BELOW A Tokyo dealer getting excited about the arrival of the 500-SS, but, with export demand already outstripping supply, folks in Japan would have to wait until the launch of the 1970 Model Year version until they could get their hands on one.

BOTTOM There were some weird and wonderful displays at the 1969 Tokyo Show, but the gold H1 was quite something. Kawasaki had 23 motorcycles on display, including four W1 variants (one of which was a police bike), and no less than seven examples of the 500-SS. (Courtesy Yaesu Publishing)

OPPOSITE PAGE The 1970 model Mach III, seen here in US trim.

LEFT Wonderful publicity shot of the domestic 1970 500-SS. Showroom models for Japan would have been fitted with ribbed Dunlop Gold Seal F2 rubber at the front, whilst retaining K77s at the rear.

BELOW Another shot from the same shoot, this one showing the alternative red paintwork offered in most markets shortly after the release of the stealth model.

Fitting into a line-up that ranged in price from 61,000 yen for the 50cc M10 all the way up to 338,000 yen for the 650cc W1S, the 298,000 yen bike was officially badged as the 500-SS in Japan (but often had the Mach III moniker applied as a suffix by dealers and the press alike), and there's no doubt the model was able to grab people's attention, especially after Kawasaki put a gold-plated version of the three in the middle of its stand! The new charcoal tank and side colouring for 1970 was also aired, joined in due course by a red option.

Show debutantes included the 100 G4TR and 350 F5 off-roaders (the GA4/90TR – a domestic version of the export-only GA3 – came too late to be included), but the rumour mill went into overdrive during the Tokyo event, with a number of sources talking about a 'Super Mach' powered by an 850cc lump delivering between 90 and 100bhp. Obviously aimed at putting the 385,000 yen CB750 in the shade, for the press was going wild over the new Honda, it wouldn't be long before something similar to this mythical creature would take a bow.

Of the other Japanese makers, Yamaha was concentrating on smaller two-strokes – more of a worry for the A1 and A7 than the W- and H-series models. The 36bhp 350R1 had evolved into the R3 by this time, duly augmented by the R3C with a raised muffler, before being replaced by the new RX line, also powered by a 350cc twin. Suzuki was like Yamaha, with smaller machines making up most of the company's sales, although the T500, launched at the 1967 Tokyo Show, had propelled the firm into another league. The T500 eventually became the basis for the GT series in 1971, when the magnificent GT750 burst onto the scene – the first of several Suzuki two-stroke triples.

On the four-stroke front, this was the time that the 53bhp XS1 launched Yamaha into the big bike arena – an ohc 653cc air-cooled twin priced at 338,000 yen, which had been rumoured since 1968. This was developed into the XS650E of 1971 vintage, and that year also saw Yamaha display its

THIS PAGE Studio pictures of the red triple for 1970, again using a US-spec bike to photograph. Note the taller cover over the CDI ignition system, introduced to improve weather sealing.

GL750-4 prototype at the Tokyo Show, so the big motorcycle movement was really heating up. In the meantime, Honda, which basically started the boom, had the sporty CB450 and CL450, with the CB500 Four following for 1971. The speed and horsepower war was in full swing. It would be interesting to see what Kawasaki would respond with. We've already hinted that Kawasaki was not resting on its laurels now the Mach III was out in all the major markets ...

Meanwhile, having claimed around ten per cent of market share in 1969 (Yamaha still had a slightly bigger piece of the cake than Kawasaki, although Honda was hogging around half of it), for the 1970 US season, Kawasaki listed the 90 G3SS and G3TR 'Bushmaster'

BELOW What has to be one of the best publicity shots ever! A Japan-spec 1970 MY 500-SS with the correct front tyre pattern for the domestic market at the time.

OPPOSITE, LEFT SIDE The American catalogue for the 1970 version of the Mach III.

BELOW The US model range brochure for the 1970 season.

models, the 100 G4TR 'Trail Boss' and G31M 'Centurion,' the 175 F3 'Bushwhacker,' the 250 F4 'Sidewinder,' A1 and A1SS 'Samurai,' the 350 F5 'Bighorn,' A7 and A7SS 'Avenger,' and the 500 H1 'Mach III'. From this list, therefore, we can see that the W-series had officially gone, and all Kawasaki machines sold in North America were powered by two-stroke engines for the 1970 season.

The 1970 Mach III, on the line at Akashi from September 1969, had a tasteful Peacock Grey livery, which looked extremely purposeful matched up with black badging

BELOW From Russia with love ... A delegation from the USSR visiting the Akashi factory. May 1970 witnessed the 500,000th bike built at Akashi leave the line.

and tank stripes. Even the headlight and the area around it was blacked-out now, so only the chrome and polished surfaces, along with the side box and oil tank badges, offered any relief from the dark shades, and even they'd been toned down compared to the originals. As 1970 proper was about to dawn, a Candy Red hue was added to the Mach III catalogue, with a white tank stripe similar in style to the dark blue one seen on the first models. By this time, the cover over the CDI distributor unit had been extended upwards to give a better seal against water ingress, and the chain was slightly thicker to prevent premature stretching, but otherwise there were no major changes outlined for the triple.

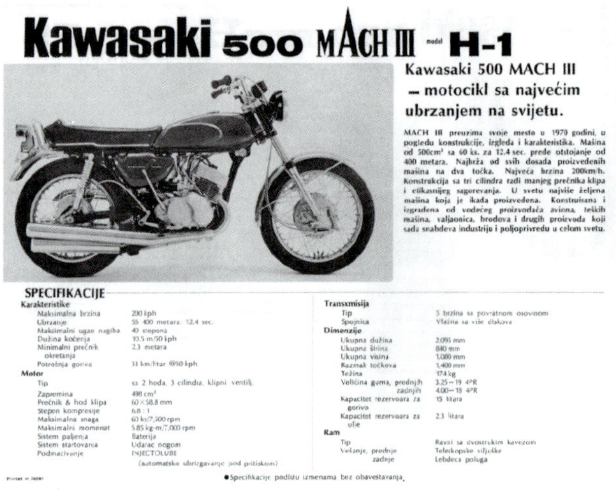

Kawasaki 500 MACH III model H-1

Kawasaki 500 MACH III – motocikl sa najvećim ubrzanjem na svijetu.

MACH III preuzima svoje mesto u 1970 godini, u pogledu konstrukcije, izgleda i karakteristika. Mašina od 500cm³ sa 60 ks. za 12.4 sec. prede otstojanje od 400 metara. Najbrža od svih dosada proizvedenih mašina na dva točka. Najveća brzina 200km/h. Konstrukcija sa tri cilindra radi manjeg prečnika klipa i efikasnijeg sagorevanja. U svetu najviše željena mašina koja je ikada proizvedena. Konstruisana i izgradena od vodećeg proizvodača aviona, teških mašina, valjaonica, brodova i drugih proizvoda koji sada snabdeva industriju i poljoprivredu u celom svetu.

SPECIFIKACIJE

Karakteristike	
Maksimalna brzina	200 kph
Ubrzanje	SS 400 metara: 12.4 sec.
Maksimalni ugao nagiba	40 stepena
Dužina kočenja	10.5 m/50 kph
Minimalni prečnik okretanja	2.3 metara
Potrošnja goriva	33 km/litar @50 kph
Motor	
Tip	sa 2 hoda, 3 cilindra, klipni ventili.
Zapremina	498 cm³
Prečnik & hod klipa	60×58.8 mm
Stepen kompresije	6.8 : 1
Maksimalna snaga	60 ks/7,500 rpm
Maksimalni momenat	5.85 kg-m/7,000 rpm
Sistem paljenja	Baterija
Sistem startovanja	Udarac nogom
Podmazivanje	INJECTOLUBE (automatsko ubrizgavanje pod pritiskom)

Transxmisija	
Tip	5 brzina sa povratnom osovinom
Spojnica	Vlažna sa više diskova
Dimenzije	
Ukupna dužina	2.095 mm
Ukupna širina	840 mm
Ukupna visina	1.080 mm
Razmak točkova	1,400 mm
Težina	174 kg
Veličina guma, prednjih	3.25–19 4PR
zadnjih	4.00–18 4PR
Kapacitet rezervoara za gorivo	15 litara
Kapacitet rezervoara za ulje	2.3 litara
Ram	
Tip	Ravni sa dvostrukim kavezom
Vešanje, prednje	Teleskopske viljuške
zadnje	Lebdeca poluga

Printed in Japan

● Specifikacije podložu izmenama bez obavestavanja.

BELOW Still with the Eastern Bloc (well, sort of) – a Mach III catalogue for Yugoslavia.

BELOW Contemporary shot of a late-1970 MY Mach III in Holland. The gold tank lettering is not standard, but looks attractive nonetheless.

Competition review: 1969-1971

Following Honda and Suzuki's lead, Yamaha duly pulled out of top-flight Grand Prix racing at the end of 1968, deciding to quit while ahead and save the huge expense of creating new engines to suit the FIM's whims, and this left the door open for Kawasaki, even though Suzuki and Yamaha continued to support a number of 'private' entries. The subtle improvements made during 1968 meant that Simmonds, despite missing the 1969 season opener in Spain due to a lack of start money, was able to go on and win in West Germany (the Hockenheim round being Kawasaki's first GP victory), the Isle of Man, Holland, Belgium, East Germany, Czechoslovakia, Finland and Italy. He scored 90 points on his KR-2, 31 more than his nearest rival (Suzuki man, Dieter Braun) and Kawasaki's faith in the Englishman's solitary efforts had been well rewarded, especially when one considers its support had often consisted of little more than a box full of bits, for that was all the race budget would allow at the time.

Simmonds was given a new six-speed gearset to suit the latest FIM regulations, along with a 'new' frame to replace the one he bent at the end of 1969, after the GP season ended, but the 125cc bike was no longer competitive in 1970, even though a fastest lap was recorded at the 1970 Isle of Man TT thanks to the Londoner. Notwithstanding, he did win at Hockenheim in 1971, but the H1-R triple was now the weapon of choice, and that was quite a different beast.

In America, Kawasaki hit the headlines thanks to its new 'racing green' livery at Daytona in 1969. Although Dick Hammer and Ken Araoka both had trouble with their 350s in the Daytona 200 classic, and Dave Simmonds and Bill Manley gave the H1 a tame debut in the same 200-miler, Harley man Cal Rayborn took fourth in the 250cc race, trapped between three Yamahas either side of him at the finish. Kawasaki's time would come, however, and the lime green warriors would become a force to be reckoned with once the men at Akashi got down to developing the H1-R triple and duly released it later in the year.

It was now becoming a familiar pattern – one that would continue until the early-1980s, as it happens. First, the road bike would be launched, then a racing version, which would duly be adopted by the works for its own competition programme. Launched at the end of 1969 in time for the 1970 season, the five-speed H1-R was perhaps the most important of all the Kawasaki road racers. This air-cooled two-stroke 498cc piston-valve machine was quoted as having 75bhp – enough to propel the brave to beyond 150mph (240kph).

The 1970 FIM Grand Prix World Championship kicked off in West Germany, but Ernst Hiller's eighth was the best Kawasaki could muster. In France, NZ rider Ginger Molloy clocked up second place for the Japanese maker, but Giacomo Agostini's MV Agusta was in a different league that year; other Kawasaki's came eighth and ninth. Now armed with an H1-R from the factory, Dave Simmonds was sixth in Yugoslavia, with another Brit, Bill Smith, claiming third as the top finisher in the sweltering heat of the Isle of Man TT classic. With a speed of 96.3mph (154.1kph), Smith was a full 5mph (8kph) off Agostini's winning pace.

Dave Simmonds claiming the spoils after winning the 1969 Dutch TT. Simmonds gave Kawasaki its first World Championship title. (Courtesy Wikimedia Commons/Dutch Nationaal Archief/Anefo)

Of the other championship races, Molloy was fourth in Holland after fuel problems, and Christian Ravel was second in Belgium, with Hiller not far behind in seventh. There were four Kawasakis in the top ten in East Germany, led home by Martin Carney in third, and while there was no 500cc race in Czechoslovakia, the races in Finland and Ireland witnessed a repeat of the French result. In Italy, Kawasaki riders came a remarkable third, fourth, fifth, sixth, eighth, ninth and tenth, and in the season finale, Molloy was second (despite Agostini staying away), Carney sixth, Ravel eighth and Simmonds ninth. With all the points added up, MV Agusta's Agostini was declared the champion, having won all ten races he entered to claim 90 points, while Molloy was runner-up on 62 (Kawasaki was second in the makers' title chase, too); Ravel was seventh on 24.

American Champion sparkplug advert from early 1969 featuring a Kawasaki racer.

Interestingly, in the early part of September 1969, Suzuki became the first maker to claim an open class victory in a US AMA national road race using a two-stroke bike, meaning Harley-Davidson, BSA and Triumph were no longer free to dominate the AMA scene at the top end, and with the H-series, the American and British manufacturers had another serious threat on its hands. Not long after, KMC announced a huge $500,000 purse being made available for winning riders using Kawasaki machines, raising the incentive for folks to move over to the Japanese brand, not only in road racing, but AMA and FIM off-road events as well, for the Bighorn was an ideal tool and Kawasaki was keen to take a bigger share of the US scrambler market, and even Bonneville.

The Kawasaki team lined up for the 1969 Daytona 200.

Anyway, the 1970 road racing season duly kicked off at Daytona in mid-March, followed by six more races before the final event at Heidelburg, PA. Daytona was the big event in the AMA calendar, of course, attracting maximum effort from the makers and maximum press coverage. Indeed, many of the AMA races were hardly covered beyond a few words in passing, while the classic Florida meeting always justified several pages in the various motorcycling publications.

After testing at FISCO, hopes were high for the H1-R in the Daytona 200, with the lightweight works-prepared bikes pumping out 80bhp, but it was not to be – Dick Mann gave the Honda 750 Four a win on its debut outing. Mark Williams was the fastest H1-R exponent, clocking 148.5mph (237.6kph) in qualifying, but Ginger Malloy was the top finisher at the end of the race, coming seventh and two laps behind the winning Honda, plus a mix of Triumph, Harley, Suzuki and Yamaha machinery; Royal Sherbet was ninth, a further lap down. At least Rusty Bradley won the 100-mile amateur race on his triple, earning himself $5000 from KMC in the process, and lessons were learnt. Next year would see a proper challenge, albeit an indirect one, with men drafted in to get the job done!

The H1-R pictured at the Akashi factory. Officially, the H1-R was quoted as having 75bhp at 9000rpm.

Rusty Bradley continued picking up the odd AMA win in the amateur category, and Hurley Wilvert was another name to watch out for. Before moving on to 1971, mention should be made of Peggy Hyde – a lady rider that made quite an impact with her Mach III Down Under, emerging from a field of 90 to win the 1970 Australian Tourist Trophy race no less, as well as a number of other events.

For 1971, the triple was modified into the H1-RAS, which was certainly fast, for those that could handle it. Dave Simmonds went a stage further, asking a UK specialist to produce a new frame made of Reynolds tubing, making the bike both lower and lighter in readiness for the 12-round FIM GP season.

Advertising announcing KMC's donation of up to $500,000 for successful Kawasaki racers in the US during 1970. For 1971, the pot was raised to $750,000 …

Giacomo Agostini took his MV Agusta to an easy victory in the season opener in Austria, but at least Kawasaki man Erick Offenstadt got onto the podium with a strong third place. Moving across the border to West Germany, Brits Ron Chandler and Maurice Hawthorne picked up third and fourth, although a fifth, thanks to Gordon Pantall, was all Kawasaki had to take away from the 500cc category in the Isle of Man TT, which was postponed due to bad weather. It was getting boring watching Agostini take the spoils, but at least Dave Simmonds gave Kawasaki fans a glimmer of hope by claiming third in the Dutch TT at Assen. Spa saw Offenstadt take second, and Chandler fifth, following a couple of Suzukis home, while the East German GP provided Ernst Hiller with a chance to shine, the German rider coming third.

There was no 500cc race in Czechoslovakia again, and the wet track in Sweden wasn't kind to the H1 runners. Simmonds got up to second in Finland, but a telling 2m19s down on Agostini. The Ulster GP, sadly marred by the troubles in Ireland, was a Suzuki benefit, but when the circus moved to Monza for the Nations GP, Giampiero Zubani took a fine second place, followed less than a second later by Simmonds. And so to Jarama in Spain on September 26, where Dave Simmonds gave Kawasaki its first 500cc Grand Prix win, with Erick Offenstadt coming third. While Agostini was once again untouchable, it should be noted that Simmonds didn't enter all the rounds, yet still finished the 1971 500cc world championship in fourth, just a few points down on the pair of Suzuki riders ahead of him; Offenstadt was sixth at the end of the year.

Interestingly, unlike Honda and Suzuki had done in the heydays of GP racing, Kawasaki put more emphasis on winning in America than it did the big events of Europe. Oddly, the Kawasaki marque was none the worse for it, for its rise in European countries had been nothing short of phenomenal, and the Stateside following was growing daily, despite some less than amazing results in US top flight competition. Imagine what sales would be like with more success on the tracks? It was a question that required an answer, and while there was no official works entry, KMC worked with 'research riders' Randy Hall and Mike Lane, giving technical feedback from the saddle. At the same time, Canadian Yvon Duhamel (an ex-Yamaha man, who was also a champion snowmobile racer and even tried his hand at NASCAR) signed for Kawasaki via Canadian dealer Fred Manley, while Rusty Bradley moved into the pro field, sponsored by Boston-based dealer John Jacobsen.

Great publicity shot prior to the 1971 Philippines Grand Prix held in Manila, showing Ken Araoka surrounded by models. The smaller Asian races were always well supported by Japanese makers, as SE Asia provided them with strong and stable markets.

For all that, it was Triumphs and BSAs that dominated the Daytona 200, despite Yvon Duhamel, Rusty Bradley, Walt Fulton and Ralph White all qualifying well, and Bob Hansen, who made his reputation with Honda, being called in as competition manager. To add insult to injury, Mike Lane was leading the 750cc race with ease, but his H1-R gave up the ghost and handed victory to Honda. As it happens, engine failures were rife that year, explaining the lack of success in the Daytona 200 (Dave Smith was the top finisher in ninth, with Cliff Carr next in a lowly 15th), and Kawasaki fans were dealt another blow when Bradley died in an accident.

At least White was third at Road Atlanta, but there were no Kawasaki men in the top ten standings at the season's halfway mark. Duhamel picked up a third at Pocono, where the Kawasaki team at last began to shine, and at Talladega, new tactics (run as hard as possible to create a gap to allow for an extra fuel stop) paid off – Duhamel won, with White following a pair of BSAs home into fourth. The Canadian was unlucky to be involved in an accident at Ontario Speedway, ruining his chances after a good first heat, and had to settle for a less than impressive 18th in the final standings at the end of the season.

Perhaps Daytona would be kind in 1972? Kawasaki entered Ken Araoka on an H1-R and Masahiro Wada on a race-prepared version of the 750cc Mach IV in the non-championship race at Fuji Speedway in September. Although Wada dropped out early on, Araoka won with ease in the pouring rain.

RIGHT Japanese advertising from late-1970, featuring the W1S and 500-SS Mach III models.

BELOW RIGHT First catalogue for the W1SA.

W1 DEVELOPMENTS

While the W-series was allowed to fade away for the US 1970 season, with only remaining stocks being sold Stateside, back home, the strict W1 was only listed until the start of 1969 (albeit in much the same manner as the US, for just a handful – quite literally! – were built in 1968), but sales of the W1S were booming, with nearly 2000 finding new homes in 1968, followed by 2759 built in 1969. Amazingly, sales were set to continue moving in the right direction, and no less than 3663 W1 Specials were produced in 1970, along with a fair few W1SP police bikes (480 over 1969 and 1970) to fatten up the numbers.

With Japan's national average wage now standing at 825,000 yen by the dawn of the seventies (almost double what it had been five years earlier), people had more money to spend on leisure pursuits. As such, big bike sales – over 350cc in Japan terms – leapt from just under 13,000 units in 1967 to around 18,000 in 1968, and increased again to about 20,000 in 1969. The Mach III was helping to swell the 1969 figures, of course, but there's no doubt the W1S had a very strong following amongst enthusiasts more interested in sport and prestige than utility.

Production at Akashi hit the 10,000 units a month milestone in March 1970, but Kawasaki was not about to rest on its laurels, though, and set about revising the W1S in order to extend its shelf life a couple of months later. The biggest change was the adoption of a 'left shift, right brake' arrangement, which was the norm in Japan and America. Indeed, the older UK-style layout had only really been kept because the remaining Meguro chaps had fought hard to retain it, saying it was a feature that added character to the bike. It's a good point, but the reality is that the newcomer would go on to have a bumper first year of sales, so perhaps there were more folks interested in ease of use (or at least a greater feeling of familiarity) than controls with additional character. At least the engineers' time and the cost of new tooling was fully justified by this show of support.

Anyway, the new W1 Special, given the W1SA moniker (with A signifying a modification), was displayed as a prototype at the 1970 Tokyo Show, which opened on October 30 that year. Interestingly, there was also a W1SA fitted with a sidecar on show. Made by Tairiku Motors of Tokyo, this W1SA and sidecar combination would duly be sold as a 658,000 yen package, although it's fair to say that it was the bike itself – priced at 348,000 yen – that grabbed the most attention.

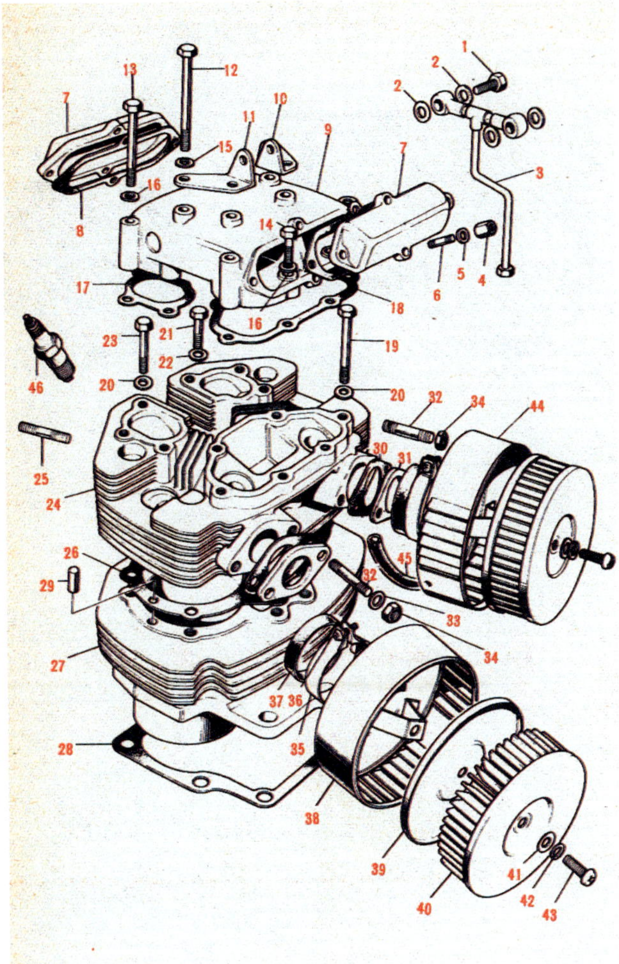

LEFT & BELOW The W1SA engine as seen in the parts book.

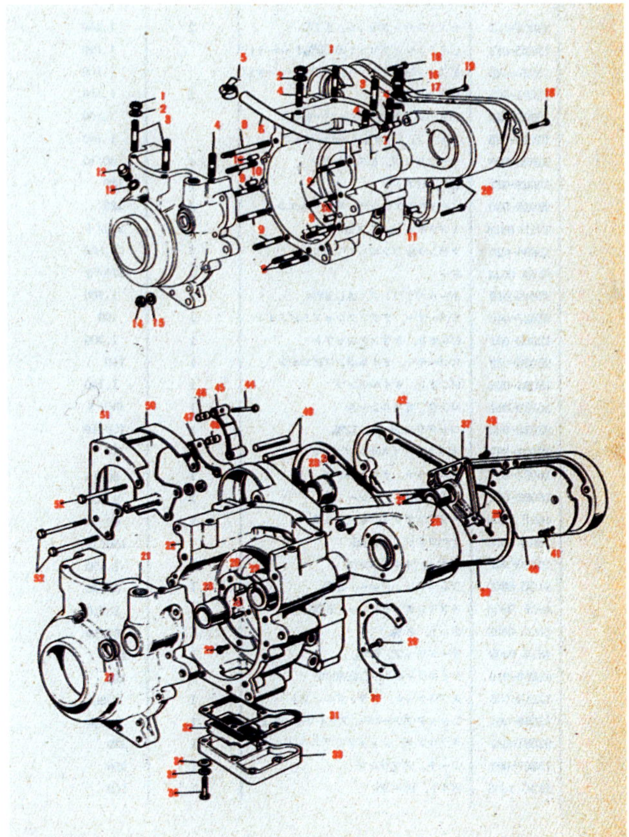

Once production began in February 1971, enthusiasts were able to spot the differences between the new and old models. Obviously a lot of engineering work had been required to change the transmission layout, but it was an excellent distinguishing feature that cannot be mistaken or readily modified (adding new parts that aren't period correct but still fit is a common occurrence, of course, especially as the years roll on, and maintenance is required), with the rear brake pedal now on the offside to match the new setup. Beyond the brake pedal, the alloy timing cover had a different logo, featuring a 'W' below the 'Kawasaki' script, while the Kawasaki name was proudly displayed on the transmission cover as well now. As a matter of interest, the change also brought about the use of new main bearings, with ball bearings at both ends of the crankshaft (replacing a roller bearing at one end, while the existing one was uprated).

The W1SA was fitted with a pair of VM28SC carburettors, which were slightly different to those found on the first W1S models, and a pair of ignition coils instead of the single one used until now. The early 'Cabton' exhaust system was carried over, however, gaining black (rather than a plain alloy finish) finned exhaust flanges as the year progressed – the 1971 Tokyo Motor Show exhibit, for example, had the early exhaust and black securing ring, which are more commonly associated with the later 'Daikon' muffler. As usual during this era, when stockpiles of certain parts were generally used up first, nothing can ever be pinned down to a uniform changeover. The only other mechanical change was the gearing, which matched that of the W2SS, meaning it was a little different to that of the original W1 Special, even though the four internal ratios were the same throughout the W-series run.

BELOW Studio shot showing the tail of an early W1SA-type W1 Special. It looked incredibly modern compared to the bike featured in the advert on page 81.

BELOW Catalogue for the 348,000 yen W1SA, with the early lighting and exhaust system.

On the cosmetic side of things, the black headlight and blacked-out area on the forks surrounding it was a feature adopted on the US 1969 Model Year W2SS, W2TT and W1SS, but there were new front indicators that were larger and flatter than before. As it happens, these indicators would continue to be employed on all home market machines all the way through to the end of the W run. Above and between them was a new set of gauges, with revised graphics, and the tachometer now placed on the right. There was also a crazy red light to warn the rider when they hit 50mph (80kph), which kind of makes having a powerful bike meaningless. But then that's Japan, making supercars when the blanket speed limit belongs in the early-1900s!

LEFT The company offered a W1SA and sidecar package, although the two components looked something of a mismatch, the sidecar lacking the modernity and elegance of the bike.

BELOW RIGHT The police version of the W1SA, known as the W1SAP. Only 207 were built, but a number were exported, including this example, bound for Mexico.

BOTTOM A W1SAP from the second half of 1971, with black paintwork and more comfortable seating than the catalogue model. Note the huge mechanical siren, which was almost a work of art.

The front mudguard was carried over, as were the wheel and tyre specs, but the brake drum gained an air scoop on the nearside, along with a black finish on the inner part of the assembly. Oddly, the offside was kept all silver, and, even stranger, it was the reverse situation on the rear drum! The rear mudguard was also the same as before, but the items surrounding it were all new – a fresh indicator unit to match those up front, a revised rear lamp with a pair of integrated reflectors, and rear dampers that featured partially exposed coil springs and were painted black at the top.

Rounding off the changes, the fuel tank was sprayed in black with either orange and white or blue and white accents, plus a 'Kawasaki' script-type badge, while the dual seat beyond it was familiar W fare. The oil tank and side box were finished in black on the W1SA, with a long '650' trim piece applied on both. All told, the bike looked far more modern than its immediate predecessor, able to fit in with the sporting image projected by the H-series, and face up to the growing competition we mentioned earlier on in the chapter that much easier.

There were other developments in other areas, with a flood of new scramblers in the early part of 1970 (the F6, F7, F8 and F81M, followed by the MT1 mini-bike), and the

THIS PAGE Japanese catalogue for the 1971 500-SS Mach III. The back cover shows a Japanese enthusiast, Yoshiaki Osako, who took a 1970 Mach III the length of the legendary Route 66 in the States. His long-distance motorcycling exploits were well-known during the late-sixties onwards.

early part of September that year seeing Kawasaki Motors Nv (KME) established in Holland – a spares company set up in conjunction with Itochu Trading to serve the European continent. The 99cc GA5 was the only other newcomer, and the only one not to have off-road ambitions, launched in November.

The 1971 version of the Mach III (given the H1A designation) was already on the line by this time, having been put into production in August 1970. The appearance was quite different, thanks to a chrome headlight, plus a smooth fuel tank profile that was easier to produce. There was 'laser blend' colouring on both fuel and oil tank, along with the side box of the Candy Blue model; '500' decals graced the oil tank and side box. Oddly, the Candy Red version, sold alongside it, retained the older badges rather than the new '500' ones, as well as a black headlight surround, and whilst the fuel tank stripe was similar to that of the 1970 model, it was now longer.

On the mechanical side of things, the front forks were modified, having a revised spring rate to soak up the bumps a little better and make the general handling feel more secure, and damping effect was increased at the rear, too, improving high-speed stability. US-bound machines, priced at $995, were also given a new tyre combination, with sticky

BELOW The US-spec Mach III for the 1971 season.

BELOW Dedicated American catalogue for the 1971 Mach III.

Dunlop K87s at the back, although K77s were retained at the front, and the sizes were still the same anyway. Following up on feedback from dealers and the field, there was a multitude of tiny changes to improve the machine's service life, such as seals, rubber mounts and so on, but nothing anyone would notice unless they were stripping a bike down and rebuilding it with new and old parts available for comparison.

Before moving on, this is as good a time as any to mention the establishment of a small R&D centre in America in April 1971, based at Santa Ana, and headed by Sid Saito. The innovative 'Jet Ski' was one of the first major projects to come out of this office, with development work beginning soon after it opened, and eventually going

BELOW The American Kawasaki range for 1971, helping to illustrate how the Mach III fitted into the Stateside line-up. Only the 250T and 350S aren't illustrated here, although things would look very different in the following season. Prices ranged from $189 to just under $1000.

BELOW MIDDLE & RIGHT Front and rear pages from an English language brochure for the Mach III triple.

BOTTOM RIGHT Newsletter cutting from the opening of the North-Central Region sales office. This was the final piece in the KMC sales network jigsaw, with the success of the regional offices allowing Kawasaki to have 1100 dealers in America by the end of 1973, three-quarters of whom were selling Kawasakis only.

North-Central Branch Grand Opening

June Cochran – "Miss Kawasaki" – snips the ribbon as company V.I.P.'s look on. Among those in the group are: Fred Vermuelen, Adm. Mgr. (far left), Alan Masek, Executive Vice President KMC (with beard), and Wayne Moulton, Vice-Pres. & Gen. Mgr., Central & N. Central regions.

on sale as the JS400 in the spring of 1973. Powered by a modified snowmobile engine (Kawasaki had just followed Yamaha's lead in this field), it was the world's first water bike, enabling people to enjoy the sensation of waterskiing without the need for a tow-boat. While we are on the subject of marine craft, for the Kawasaki enthusiast with everything, the company displayed a jet boat at the 1972 Osaka Boat Show, which made quite an impact.

Meanwhile, there was also the first of five US regional offices established, helping make dealers feel they had a greater level of contact with KMC than a centralized system could offer. These would handle sales, marketing, parts distribution and technical services, with the first opening Georgia in 1971 (South Region Sales), followed by Texas (Central Region Sales) in the following year, and Minnesota (North-Central Region Sales) in 1973. Of course, KMC head office looked after the west, while the east coast was in the care of the long-standing New Jersey offices.

BELOW The French were always very keen on the Kawasaki marque. The H1, A7, A1 and GA2A are illustrated here as Les Grandes Routières.

A tour of the Akashi factory

A pictorial journey through the Akashi factory in mid-1971. Pictures show the S2 on the line, machining, checking tolerances, building up the bottom-end of a triple, frame welding, line work on a 750cc H2 (note the 'Kawasaki' logo used on this model), fuel tank painting, completed Mach IVs for export (only blue was listed initially, with gold added mid-season), and a Mach II on the test course.

BELOW Styling mock-up of the 350cc Mach II. Other prototypes displayed seating like the old Raleigh Chopper, but thankfully good taste was allowed to prevail, and the production version was toned down by a fair amount.

MACH LINE ADDITIONS

Kawasaki policy was becoming clearer and clearer with each passing year – sporting two-stroke road machines and a line of rugged, increasingly powerful scrambler models, ably backed up by the W-series in the home market, as the golden oldie had a remarkably strong following in its native land. How long the company could persist with two-stroke engines was a question on everyone's lips, as it was quite simply a matter of time before ever-tighter emission regulations caught up with this technology. There was still a little while before the EPA and others like it had the final say, though, and – almost as a sign of defiance – both Kawasaki and Suzuki introduced some spectacular two-stroke machines as the seventies progressed ...

With the Mach III thriving, its sheer speed having well and truly poked Honda and other rivals in the eye, it was time to expand the line of two-stroke Kawasaki air-cooled triples, with a smaller model given priority, thanks to its greater sales potential in all markets; particularly at home.

BELOW European version of the S2 with low handlebars, and the rear mudguard required by European countries.

BELOW Japanese advertising for the 228,000 yen 350-SS, with the red version of the 1971 500-SS in the background. Red paintwork was the norm for the 350-SS, with a white option added later on.

Production of the racy-looking 350 S2 (also known as the Mach II or 350-SS) began in January 1971. The concept followed that of the H1, with the all-alloy three-cylinder engine placed in a welded double-cradle tubular frame, but with a 53mm bore and 52.3mm stroke for the S2, the cubic capacity was reduced to 346cc, while the exhausts were more upswept at the rear giving the new bike a distinctly sporting appearance. Smaller VM24SC carburettors were employed, and the CDI ignition was ditched in order to keep costs in check. With a 7.3:1 c/r, the unit developed 45bhp at 8000rpm – enough to propel the 149kg (328lb) machine to a 13.6 second standing-quarter before going on to a 112mph (179kph) top speed.

The five-speed constant mesh transmission was interesting in that it adopted a 'one down, four up' pattern, which was unusual at the time for Kawasaki, even though it was the accepted norm amongst many other makers. Drum brakes were fitted at both ends, which were more than enough given the bike's performance and weight. The modern front mudguard was made of painted steel, covering narrow 3.00-18 rubber, while the back used a simple tail cowling not found on the H1; a chrome rear mudguard was necessary for Europe, though, draped over a 3.50-18 tyre. Indicators were fitted as standard for all markets, although US-bound machines still required additional side reflectors. Rounding things off, a pair of anti-glare instruments was mounted above the black headlight.

With development having started in 1968, pilot production of the 750 H2 (also known as the Mach IV or 750-SS) began in January 1971 alongside the S2, although it would be some time before it reached the showrooms. While the S2 (Mach II) was available in Japan from the spring, it was not listed in America until the 1972 season. With the H2, it was a reverse scenario, with the same release timing as the S2 chosen for the bigger machine in the States, with domestic sales following a couple of months later, in November 1971. From this we can conclude that even though Japan was experiencing a big bike boom, it was still smaller-capacity models that sold in volume, while the US placed more importance on the heavyweight classes. There was also the AMA Formula 750 race category to think about, and the relevance a quick entry in that Class would have for American enthusiasts. Indeed, in retrospect, we can almost consider the Mach IV as a homologation special ...

Anyone that has followed the story thus far will be familiar with the technical details, for this was basically a

LEFT An H2 styling mock-up. Design work associated with the frame and body parts was handled by Toshio Togashi and Keisuke Tomonaga in the main.

BELOW Early brochure for the Mach IV illustrated all the leading features of the new bike.

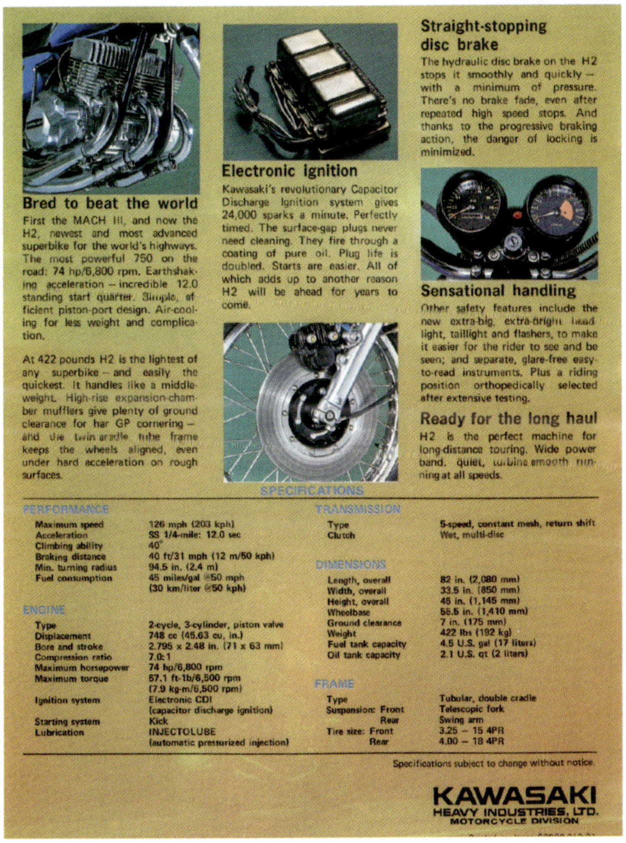

Bred to beat the world

First the MACH III, and now the H2, newest and most advanced superbike for the world's highways. The most powerful 750 on the road: 74 hp/6,800 rpm. Earthshaking acceleration – incredible 12.0 standing start quarter. Simple, efficient piston-port design. Air-cooling for less weight and complication.

At 422 pounds H2 is the lightest of any superbike – and easily the quickest. It handles like a middleweight. High-rise expansion-chamber mufflers give plenty of ground clearance for har GP cornering – and the twin cradle tube frame keeps the wheels aligned, even under hard acceleration on rough surfaces.

Electronic ignition

Kawasaki's revolutionary Capacitor Discharge Ignition system gives 24,000 sparks a minute. Perfectly timed. The surface-gap plugs never need cleaning. They fire through a coating of pure oil. Plug life is doubled. Starts are easier. All of which adds up to another reason H2 will be ahead for years to come.

Straight-stopping disc brake

The hydraulic disc brake on the H2 stops it smoothly and quickly – with a minimum of pressure. There's no brake fade, even after repeated high speed stops. And thanks to the progressive braking action, the danger of locking is minimized.

Sensational handling

Other safety features include the new extra-big, extra-bright head light, taillight and flashers, to make it easier for the rider to see and be seen; and separate, glare-free easy-to-read instruments. Plus a riding position orthopedically selected after extensive testing.

Ready for the long haul

H2 is the perfect machine for long-distance touring. Wide power band, quiet, turbine-smooth running at all speeds.

SPECIFICATIONS

PERFORMANCE

Maximum speed	126 mph (203 kph)
Acceleration	SS 1/4-mile: 12.0 sec
Climbing ability	40°
Braking distance	40 ft/31 mph (12 m/50 kph)
Min. turning radius	94.5 in. (2.4 m)
Fuel consumption	45 miles/gal @50 mph (30 km/liter @50 kph)

ENGINE

Type	2-cycle, 3-cylinder, piston valve
Displacement	748 cc (45.63 cu, in.)
Bore and stroke	2.795 x 2.48 in. (71 x 63 mm)
Compression ratio	7.0:1
Maximum horsepower	74 hp/6,800 rpm
Maximum torque	57.1 ft-1b/6,500 rpm (7.9 kg-m/6,500 rpm)
Ignition system	Electronic CDI (capacitor discharge ignition)
Starting system	Kick
Lubrication	INJECTOLUBE (automatic pressurized injection)

TRANSMISSION

Type	5-speed, constant mesh, return shift
Clutch	Wet, multi-disc

DIMENSIONS

Length, overall	82 in. (2,080 mm)
Width, overall	33.5 in. (850 mm)
Height, overall	45 in. (1,145 mm)
Wheelbase	55.5 in. (1,410 mm)
Ground clearance	7 in. (175 mm)
Weight	422 lbs (192 kg)
Fuel tank capacity	4.5 U.S. gal (17 liters)
Oil tank capacity	2.1 U.S. qt (2 liters)

FRAME

Type	Tubular, double cradle
Suspension: Front	Telescopic fork
Rear	Swing arm
Tire size: Front	3.25 – 15 4PR
Rear	4.00 – 18 4PR

Specifications subject to change without notice.

KAWASAKI
HEAVY INDUSTRIES, LTD.
MOTORCYCLE DIVISION

748cc version of the Mach III, powered by a two-stroke air-cooled piston-valve triple. The larger displacement was gained via enlarging both the bore and stroke (upped to 71mm x 63mm) in fresh, scaled-up castings made specifically for the job under Matsumoto-san's guidance, and with a 7.0:1 compression ratio, new high-silicon pistons, a simplified magneto CDI ignition system (an expense much

RIGHT Although side markers were standard in Japan, at least on the H2, the seat strap was not necessary on US-bound machines, as the chrome bar behind the seat met Federal regulations for pillion passengers. The domestic badging, as mentioned in the text, confirms that this is indeed a Japan-spec model.

MIDDLE The US-spec 750 H2 Mach IV viewed from the opposite side.

BOTTOM Catalogue pages featuring a European-spec H2.

easier to justify on a flagship model, especially as it saved weight as well), a bank of Mikuni VM30SC carburettors and 'Injectolube,' the unit was quoted as delivering 74bhp at 6800rpm, along with 57lbft of torque at 6500rpm.

The five-speed transmission (with neutral at the bottom) came with a primary reduction ratio of 1.88, and a final reduction of 3.13. Mated to cogs giving 2.17 on first, 1.47 on second, 1.11 on third, 0.92 on fourth and 0.81 on fifth, this endowed the H2 with a 126mph (202kph) top speed. According to the catalogue, it would dismiss the standing-quarter in 12 seconds dead, making it the fastest production motorcycle in the world at that time.

Interestingly, the H2 followed the styling cues of Norimasa Tada's S2 rather than the H1, which would duly be updated to match the newcomers for the 1972 Model Year. As such, we can see features like the painted front mudguard (the rear chrome one was only standard in Europe again), the big lights, glare-free gauges, the upswept seat to flow into the metal cowl surrounding the rear light, and the sharper angle on the separated exhaust pipes. Even the tank stripes were similar, continuing through to the back of the bike, and the badging, too, at least in export markets. Early Japanese models had a hefty 'Mach III 750' badge on the oil tank and side box, which is extremely odd, seeing as it was a Mach IV! It does sort of confirm the III representing triple, but maybe not. Anyway, a 'Mach III 500' version of the badge was used on the 1972 domestic H1 as well, but only for that season, while it faded out on the H2 midway through the 1973 season.

There were some notable changes made for the 192kg (422lb) 750cc machine, however, not least the adoption of hydraulic disc braking up front, with just a single disc on the nearside of the hub to keep weight in check, although double discs were available as an option; the rear drums were increased in diameter at the same time. The front forks, with steering damper, were uprated to a larger diameter,

BELOW The Mach IV for the European market, with the same badging as the US machine, but no side reflector at the front. The majority of European countries also called for a seat strap to be provided for passenger use, even though many users complained they were as good as useless in the real world.

and the tyre sizes aped those of the 500cc Mach III. Even then, Yokohama rubber was chosen for the Mach IV, with the same rear tyre for all markets, combined with either a ribbed Y-980 tyre (for Japan) or a Y-623 tread pattern for America and other foreign destinations; some distributors chose a Dunlop K77 for the front on early models, by the way, just to add to the confusion. The frame was reinforced with heavier-gauge tubing and extra bracing, as was the rear swing arm, and a manual chain oiler was an interesting addition.

Dan Hunt attended the US press launch based on the *Queen Mary*, berthed at Long Beach. He noted that despite the H2's softer state of tune compared to the H1 (Mach III): "As expected, the Mach IV is an absolute jet, leaves all sorts of rubber on the pavement, pulls strongly in every gear, and shows absolutely no lag as you click your way from first to fifth."

The Mach range of two-stroke triples was duly completed by the 250 S1/KH250A (or Mach I), the first of which began rolling down the Akashi production line in March 1971. This was a 250cc version of the S2, with the same piston-valve lump, but a smaller 45mm bore to give a fresh displacement of 249cc.

Coming with three VM22SC carburettors, a 7.5:1 c/r and coil-and-battery ignition, the S1 delivered 32bhp at 8000rpm, which, in a bike weighing only 148kg (326lb), gave it more than adequate performance. The five-speed gearbox had the same selection pattern as the 350cc bike, meaning the S-series as a whole employed the 'one down, four up' sequence, while the pair in the H-series kept neutral at the bottom. With the same styling features as the S2, it used drum brakes at both ends, and the same front tyre as its sister model, but matched with narrower 3.25-18 rubber at the rear.

Lining up alongside the 350 F9, G5/KE100A and F11/KE250A scramblers as newcomers at the 1971 Tokyo Show, the 250 S1 was released in Japan as the 218,000

BELOW LEFT English language catalogue for the 250 S1 triple, also known as the Mach I. It was sold in Europe and Australia initially, as well as Japan.

BELOW RIGHT American advertising from the time of the Mach IV's launch.

OPPOSITE, LEFT The Mach II, III and IV were the three stars highlighted in KMC's 'Tri-Star' advertising – the Tri-Star reference doubtless making the most of the stir caused by the new Lockheed aircraft. The fourth star in the equation, the Mach I, was deemed too late for the US 1972 season, and was not available Stateside until the 1973 Model Year.

yen 250-SS in February 1972. Being only 10,000 yen cheaper than the 350-SS, this must have caused headaches for dealers and buyers alike, but at least there was a lot of daylight between the S-series and the 500-SS, and the exotic 365,000 yen H2.

Incidentally, the 1972 Model Year 500-SS (Mach III) was also displayed at the 1971 Tokyo Show. Now priced at 305,000 yen, it came with a host of modifications to justify the increase. As well as new colouring to match the H2 and S-series (including the tank stripes, modern painted mudguards, both front and rear on the H1, and black headlight), the 1972 H1 had an H2-type front fork and

BELOW A 500 H1 Mach III for Europe, with low handlebars and a ribbed front tyre, the latter also being employed in Japan. Not all European markets required dual reflectors, but some did; headlight specifications also varied across the continent.

disc brake arrangement (a timely move, seeing as several magazines had noted the old brakes could only just keep up with the 500's blistering pace), and a new steering damper. An interesting change was the adoption of the European ignition system in all markets (bikes with this were given the H1B designation), although CDI was available for those that wanted it (these models were known as the H1C version in parts books); either way, the carburettor jetting was revised, bringing the VM28SC KA4 into play on the H1B and KA5 on the H1C. It also came with a bigger taillight and larger side reflectors, polished end covers on the engine, plus a new 'Mach III 500' badge for the home market.

BOTTOM LEFT Japanese advert from early 1972. Note the badge on the oil tank, which was based on the 750 one in the domestic market.

BELOW English language brochure for the 1972 MY version of the Mach III.

BOTTOM RIGHT The US-spec Mach III for the 1972 season.

OPPOSITE TOP Two views of the W1 Special, or W1SA, in the same format it was displayed at the 1971 Tokyo Show.

BELOW While the American PR campaign was all 'Space Age' and glitz, domestic brochures had a completely different atmosphere about them, such as this one for the tiny 100 GA5-A road bike.

BOTTOM Japanese advertising announcing the arrival of the 750SS.

H-series timeline

A summary of major H-series developments, putting things into chronological order. For leading specifications and production numbers, please refer to Appendix II.

- September 1968 – pilot production of the H1/KH500A begins at Akashi.
- January 1969 – sales of the H1 begin in America, where it uses the Mach III moniker. Priced at $999, it picks up the "rocket with a sprocket" nickname.
- September 1969 – release of the 298,000 yen H1 in Japan, where it is badged as the 500-SS.
- December 1969 – the 75bhp H1-R production racer goes on sale.
- January 1971 – pilot production of the H2 starts at the Akashi factory, built alongside the new S2 (Mach II) triple, and soon the S1 (Mach I), completing the Mach line-up.
- September 1971 – sales of the $1386 H2 begin in the USA, where it officially uses the 750 Mach IV H2 nameplate.
- November 1971 – domestic sales of the 365,000 yen H2 begin, using the 750-SS name.
- March 1973 – the 100bhp H2-R production racer is released for general sale.
- July 1973 – pilot production of the S3 begins, replacing the S2 for the 1974 season. Sold in Japan as the 400-SS from January 1974.
- 1976 MY – global sales of H2 end before the 1976 season begins (Japan had lost the big triple much earlier), and the H1 is replaced by a new KH500 grade. At the same time, the KH250 and KH400 names are adopted for the S1 and S3.

While the W1 Special on display at the 1971 Tokyo Show was still an early type machine, soon after, the W1SA's exhaust system was changed for one with a 'Daikon' silencer that would provide quieter running; black exhaust flanges secured the pipes to the head. The rear indicators were moved a fraction back and higher up at the same time (or on special fixings when optional panniers were fitted), providing another means of identification.

Kawasaki's Tokyo Show stand may have been dominated by two-stroke machines, with the W1 looking a little out of place, but storm clouds were looming for makers of bikes with these engines. The next chapter looks at how Kawasaki not only came up with a motorcycle that would ultimately take over the W-series mantle, it would combine the latter's refinement with the electrifying pace of the company's triples to create a true superbike ...

4 THE FIRST Z-SERIES MACHINES

The Z was an important machine in so many ways, with the refined power expected of a touring bike, and enough pace so as not to be embarrassed by the manic Mach line. It was true reflection of the company, which had by now matured into a motorcycle manufacturer of world renown – no compromises, and no excuses necessary ...

LEFT Cover and inner pages from a 1972 Mach III catalogue, with an American-spec model in the main illustration. After all, the USA was the biggest market by far for the H-series triples.

The 1972 Model Year was an important one for Kawasaki, signalling a modernization of the range – a new era. American enthusiasts had the 350 Mach II, 500 Mach III and 750 Mach IV road bikes, plus the 90 G3, 100 G4, 100 G5, 125 F6, 175 F7, 250 F8 and 350 F9 scramblers to choose from. Those long-running A1 and A7 variants had gone at last – at least in the States! It was an impressive line-up clearly reflecting Kawasaki's sporting image.

The policy was less clear-cut in Japan, with the price list from spring 1972 having the Kawasaki 90 at 76,000 yen, the 90SS at 79,000 yen (or 82,000 yen in DX guise), the 90SSS at the same price as the 90SS DX, and the 90TR at 94,000 yen; the strict 90SS and 90SSS wouldn't be around much longer, however. Then there was the old-fashioned 125B at 135,000 yen, and the 125TR scrambler at 153,000 yen.

The 250 range included the A1 Special at 187,000 yen, the A1SS Special at 192,000 yen, the 250-SS (S1) at 218,000 yen, and 250TR at 195,000 yen, so the A1 was still alive and well, even though having only the 228,000 yen 350-SS (S2) and 225,000 yen 350TR listed in the 350 category meant the A7 had fallen by the wayside in Japan, too; by the summer, the A1 variants had gone from price lists once and for all. The A1 and A7 had certainly had a good run, serving the company well. According to factory figures, 20,523 regular A1s were built as 1970 came to a close, along with 10,664

LEFT The 1972 Mach IV, also in US guise.

BELOW LEFT A Japanese dealer advertising the 750-SS (or Mach IV), as well as the 350-SS (or S2), the 500-SS (H2) and 650cc W1 Special. The 250cc triple had yet to arrive on the scene.

BELOW The 32bhp 250 S1 at the time of its debut. Domestic sales began in February 1972, with the 250-SS name being adopted in Japan. Other than the badging, it looked much the same as the 350 S2, and was continued in this guise in a number of markets into the 1973 season. In some places, like France, the 1972 S2 was also carried over into the 1973 line-up.

A1SS models. In addition, 17,800 A7s and 6856 A7SS grades were produced.

Finally, there was the 500-SS (H1) at 305,000 yen, the 650 W1 Special at 348,000 yen, and the 750-SS (H2) model at 365,000 yen. To put these prices into perspective, the contemporary Suzuki GT250 was 197,000 yen, while the GT750 was 385,000 yen – the same as a Honda CB750 Four. Yamaha's peppy RX350 was punted at 216,000 yen, while the XS650 commanded 365,000 yen. A few months later, Yamaha would add the 385,000 yen TX750 to its range, meaning all members of the Japanese 'Big Four' were now fielding 750cc bikes. The other three were also selling a huge range of 50cc, 60cc and 70cc machines, diluting their

BELOW LEFT The 1972 Model Year W1SA, still with the ten-fin head at this stage, although the 'Daikon' mufflers are a good distinguishing feature for dating.

BOTTOM RIGHT AND OPPOSITE LEFT Groovy (always wanted to use that word!) Japanese advertising from the summer of 1972 featuring the W1 Special, or W1SA.

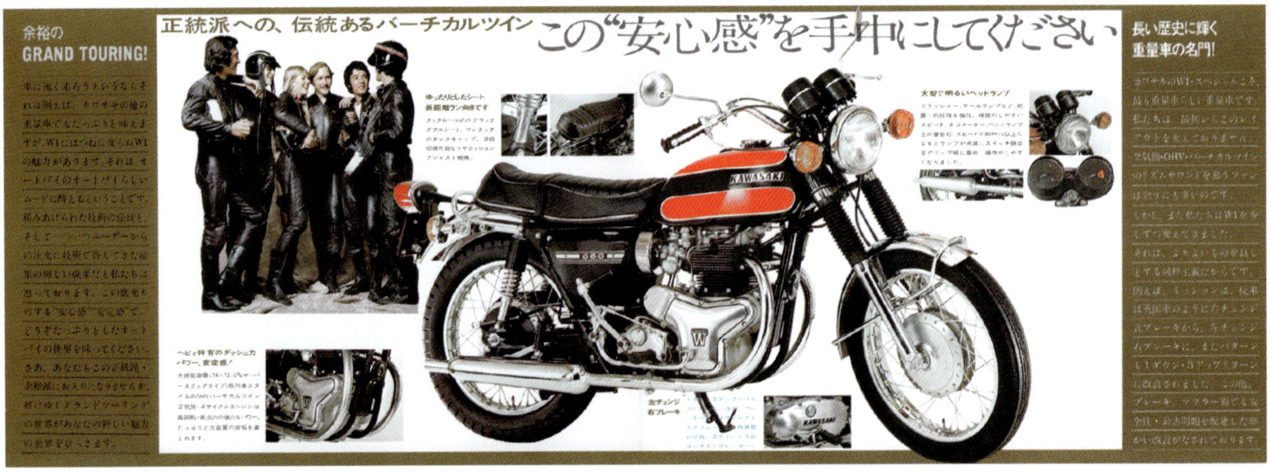

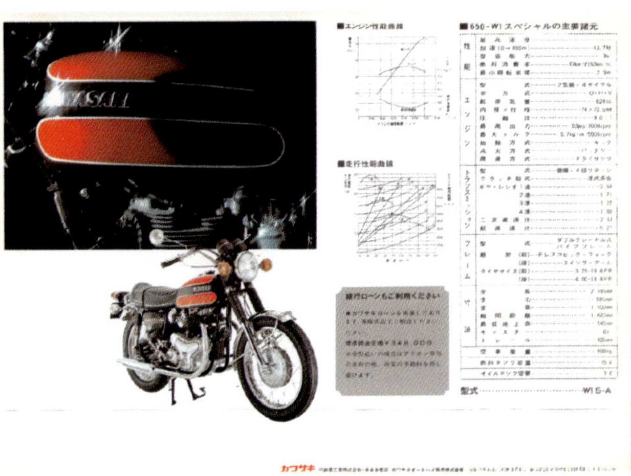

sporting credentials somewhat, but that challenge at the top-end could not be ignored. Fortunately, Kawasaki already had an answer waiting in the wings – the Z1 …

A NEW FLAGSHIP

The world was no longer the carefree place it once was. Emissions regulations had caught up with cars and motorcycles, as industrial cities choked on smog and other gunk in the air. The two-stroke may have been king for the racing fraternity and ton-up boys, but it was the enemy of the EPA and tree lovers, and California wanted an end to the noise these rorty beasts made, too. It wasn't just America attacking Kawasaki's livelihood, though, as Japan's Ministry of the Environment brought in stricter rules on emissions in December 1972, aping those of the Muskie Act in the States. It was a death knell for large two-stroke machines, or at the very least, a heavy flesh wound that would have to be tended to. As well as facing the threat posed by the other Japanese makers in the big bike class, Kawasaki had to move with the times.

That Kawasaki was working on a bike to beat the Honda CB750 came as a surprise to no-one. Reports were circulating in the press about a V4 on test as early as mid-1970, with engineers doubtless trying to salvage something from the doomed 1967 racer project. There was even a two-stroke square-four on the drawing board in 1972, proving that the company was not quite ready to give up on two-stroke engines just yet. However, to fight both the CB and Federal regulations head-on (for the US market was always going to be the main outlet), there was only one sensible conclusion – a four-stroke machine was needed.

BOTTOM RIGHT A Z1 at speed at the JARI test site. The Vietnam War was still on everyone's mind in America, and the Watergate scandal was just kicking off, too, but at least Kawasaki fans had something to look forward to …

BELOW RIGHT The final styling mock-up of the T103 (or Z1) that was shipped to America for appraisal, pictured back at Akashi in May 1971. The '749' badge on the tank was out of place, for a 903cc engine capacity had already been decided on, while the colouring and graphics were still to be looked at in detail. Most of the Keisuke Tomonaga-designed body was made of wood, although the engine is an early prototype. The lines for the production machine were penned by Norimasa Tada, however.

OPPOSITE LEFT Colour and graphics proposals for the T103 project, dated 1972.

Yukio Otsuki was placed in overall charge of the new big bike project, given the internal codename of 'New York Steak' in its final stages, with Junichi Watanabe looking after the day-to-day proceedings. Incidentally, the steak nomenclature – somehow rather fitting for something that, badged as the Z1, would ultimately become the largest displacement motorcycle ever fielded by a Japanese maker at the time – actually came about as a joke from Osamu 'Sam' Tanegashima, who looked after all the original concept research.

As it happens, the route to the Z1 was a convoluted one, delayed and reappraised in light of Honda releasing the 750cc four that led the way and duly set the bench mark, throwing the British twins and others into the shade overnight. Here was an exotic bike, up there with the MV Agusta 600, for instance, but built for the masses, and with modern styling to boot.

The Z1's roots can be traced back to the N600 project, which kicked off in April 1967 in the form of a study group on future four-stroke engine design, evolving into thoughts on the creation of a completely new machine that could take on and beat the Nortons, BSAs and Triumphs that were selling so well in the States by the following spring. Interestingly, the twin-cam Hondas of the era were considered to be lacking in torque, so it was the larger-engined British machines that were in Kawasaki's sights. Cutting vibration was put at the top of the agenda, which was hardly a surprise given the company's experience with the W-series in America, with usability, reliability and servicing ease being a matter of course.

The N600 project had reached the mock-up stage, but following the CB750 launch, chaos reigned, and everything was put on hold to enable all those concerned to re-evaluate the situation. By the summer of 1969, meetings were held on both sides of the Pacific to firm-up ideas on the N600, with Otsuki finally being given a green light to develop a new T103 project instead. The original concept of an air-cooled, transverse-mounted four-cylinder dohc unit – using the technology of the W-series, the stillborn Kei-car engine, and the best the competition had to offer – was duly built on by Gyoichi Inamura (Kawasaki's four-stroke specialist) and his small team, with the cubic capacity going up from 750cc to 900cc in an unbridled display of oneupmanship. As if that wasn't enough, the top secret plans called for the ability to increase the engine's capacity up to 1200cc with ease.

The first prototype engines were completed at the end of 1970. Soon after, a mock-up was shown to the KMC staff in America, for final input on the styling and any other thoughts. The relationship between the US arm and the chaps back in Akashi was not always smooth, as it happens, with stubborn pride showing through on both sides, but this is where Otsuki excelled, being able to listen to all the arguments and allow things to move forward.

Next up, following a lengthy period of parts sourcing and tooling up (sand casting was used to make earliest casings), the first complete prototype bikes were produced

RIGHT Close to production status, Tomonaga and Tada were still trying out various stripe designs. This is actually the same bike with different graphics on each side, and a slightly shorter wheelbase than the showroom model.

BOTTOM RIGHT Akihiko 'Kiyo' Kiyohara putting one of the seven T103 prototypes through its paces in 1971. Note the Honda helmet, which would have deflected attention a little, for the four-cylinder project was still very much a secret at this stage.

during November 1971 to allow a full testing programme to begin in earnest. These sessions, conducted on regular roads as well as the Yatabe and Tsukuba tracks, brought to light a number of niggling problems, which were duly sorted one by one, allowing two pre-production models to be sent to the States in early 1972 for more tests in their main market environment.

Z1 pilot production

A superb sequence of photographs showing the Z1 in the pilot production stage, allowing engineering staff and those on the line to iron out problems before mass-production begins – a system that ensures build quality and worker efficiency. The pictures show the engine being built up, the four-cylinder unit being mounted in the frame, frame components being added, final assembly, and customising in the test bay ...

BELOW RIGHT A sectioned display engine showing the internal workings of the Z1 powerplant. The unit was as visually striking as it was smooth and powerful, with the black paint being used to make it look different to the Honda four.

BOTTOM RIGHT The magnificent engine in situ, with this angle perfectly showing off the separate exhaust pipes and the contrast provided by combining painted and polished surfaces. Note the proud '903cc' marking on a block below the right-hand exhaust. Later in the year, 'Kickstart' was embossed on the lever mounting, satisfying America's fetish for labels.

Z1 PRODUCTION MODELS

The end result of the T103 project was the Z1, or KZ900A to give it its full title. At the heart of the beast was an air-cooled, four-stroke four-cylinder powerplant mounted across the frame in a transverse fashion. The all-alloy unit had a nine-piece built-up crankshaft with needle roller bearings for both the six mains (only the two at each end could be replaced, as the crank was supplied as an assembly) and the conrod big-ends. These bearings were considered worth the extra expense on a number of counts, and indeed, throughout the engine's design, whenever there was a question of cost versus reliability, reliability was always given priority.

A 66mm x 66mm bore and stroke was chosen, giving a 903cc displacement. The head featured double-overhead camshafts, which was a real rarity on a motorcycle, despite the efficiency benefits. With two valves (36mm/1.4in diameter inlets, and 30mm/1.2in across for the exhaust valves) per pot, the cam timing was actually very mild, making the machine more useable on a daily basis, although the dohc arrangement left plenty of scope for tuning. At the end of the day, the concept called for a combination of performance, refinement and comfort – a true GT, rather than a racer in disguise. Continuing the practical theme, the engine was kept as compact as possible to help the rider get a good seating position, with the central camshaft drive chain serving as a good example of this train of thought, along with the ancillary drive.

With four Mikuni VM28SC carburettors, an 8.5:1 compression ratio, a conventional 12V battery and coil ignition (with two sets of points), and separate upswept exhausts for each cylinder, the wet sump unit produced a healthy 82bhp at 8500rpm (500rpm off the red line), along with 54lbft of torque. It was friendly to the environment, too, with a PCV (positive crankcase ventilation) system that reduced HC emissions by as much as 40 per cent, and quiet enough to pass all US noise regulations with ease. In

LEFT Studio images showing the front, side and tail of the new Z1, as well as an interesting shot that gives us a clear view of the Nippon Denso instruments, with the speedo marked up to 160mph or 240kph depending on the market. All warning lights were contained in the panel between the speedometer and 12,000rpm tachometer. By the way, the side view shows a short rear mudguard, while the one in the tail shot is the longer European version.

BOTTOM A Z1 fresh off the line, located in the site 24 building.

addition, the valve seats were hardened to allow the bike to run on cleaner lead-free fuel without concern.

The transmission was contained within the horizontally-split crankcases – a five-speed gearbox with a 'one down, four up' shift on the nearside (the rider's left). Drive was via a hefty clutch plus a traditional chain setup with an automatic oiler rather than a shaft, something that was slowly becoming more and more popular at the top end of the market. The ratios gave a 12-second standing-quarter time, and a top speed in excess of 125mph (200kph).

The strong yet light double-loop frame, made of mild steel tubing, and the various components attached to it were well up to the job of harnessing such performance thanks to the vast experience of Toshio Togashi. The telescopic fork up front was prepared for a dual disc setup (a single brake disc was standard, with a front pair listed as optional), and the swing-arm rear suspension came with adjustable shocks. The drum at the rear (activated by a pedal on the offside, next to the kickstart lever placed there as a back-up to the electric starter) was never questioned, or the lack of a steering damper for that matter. Rounding things off, Dunlop supplied the K87 4.00-18 rubber at the rear, along with a new K103 3.25-19 ribbed tyre for the front.

The styling was clean and modern, with brightwork

BELOW Scene from the international press gathering staged at Akashi in June 1972, and a German advert announcing the world debut of the Z1, or the Kawasaki 900 Super 4 as it was known in Europe.

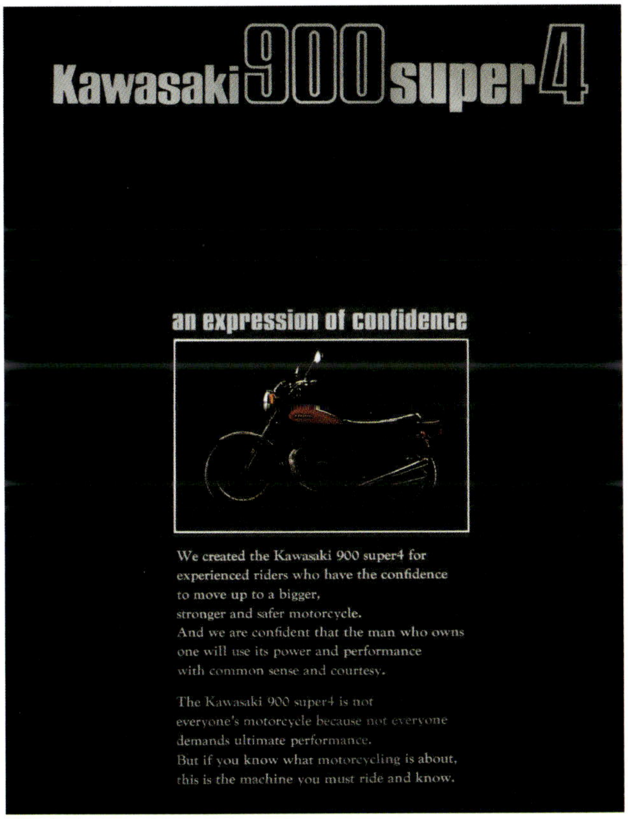

BELOW & BOTTOM The catalogue that was handed out at the IMFA event, minus the spec sheet page. The American catalogue was a much grander publication, although many of the pictures contained in it are reproduced in this section of the book anyway.

kept to a minimum (even areas of the engine were painted black!), an elegant fuel tank with a hinged dual seat beyond, giving access to the bike's electrics, a tail section inspired by the Mach line, and compact side trim, made possible by the wet sump lubrication. The colouring also helped add an air of sophistication, with dark brown being matched with orange graphics (some will say red, as it was actually the reddish-orange shu hue found in Japanese shrines and so on), and dark green with yellow.

Pilot production began at Akashi in May 1972, allowing a final test programme to be instigated, with international press members invited to Japan in the following

BELOW The 1972 Tokyo Show stand, featuring a Z1 fitted with optional touring equipment. For those wondering, the girl was definitely not on the option list! This particular bike was shod with Dunlop F6s up front. The author has also seen F11s in press pictures, although a new K103 tyre was fitted on production models.

BOTTOM The Z1 sharing the cover of *Cycle World* with a Munch 1200 TTS.

BELOW Fascinating pictures taken during the making of a dealer training film, made internally and dubbed in numerous languages to suit various markets.

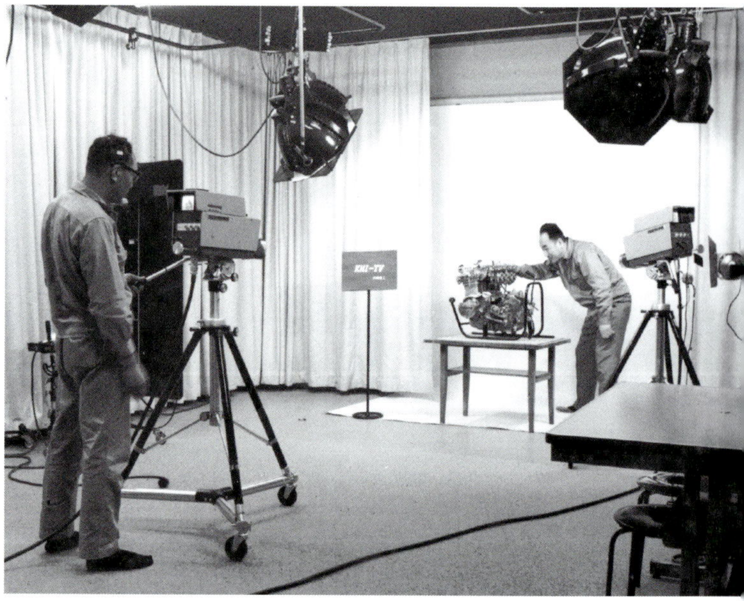

month in order to get as much coverage as possible in plenty of time for the 1973 season. Most magazine articles came out just as the bike made its official debut as the Kawasaki 900 Super 4 (the Z1's European name) at the 1972 Cologne Show, or IFMA as it was also known, which opened on September 16 that year. It then did the rounds in America, badged as the 900 Z1, as well as putting in appearances at the Paris Salon and Tokyo Motor Show, even though the Z1 was not available for the domestic market. We'll get to that particular part of the story in a moment ...

But it was the American market that the Z1 was produced for, and the early signs were good. Initially selling for $1895, *Cycle World* noted in its first proper test: "Riding the Z1 is a thrill that can hardly be described. Withdraw the clutch lever, snick the gearlever down into low gear, and prepare to experience the smoothest trip ever. Due to its mild state of tune, the Z1 can be made to pull from 1000rpm up without hesitation or bucking. Good power comes on as low as 2500rpm and doesn't fall off until well past 8500rpm. This is truly one of the most flexible machines we've ever

BELOW A new prototype shop (the site 36 building) was opened at Akashi in February 1972, followed four months later by a four-stroke engine line situated in the site 39 building. Later in the year, the noise and pollution testing facilities were expanded, which was a definite sign of the times. This picture of the Akashi works was taken at the end of 1973, incidentally, when a second test course lane was added alongside the old one.

BOTTOM Publicity shot for the 1973 MY Z1 in European guise.

BELOW A rare green and yellow Z1, seen here in European spec. Series-production models for Europe generally had no reflectors on the fork, combined with rear shocks without a reflector base (this early publicity shot has the US damper unit with the reflector removed). They also had a longer rear mudguard, and a strap for pillion passengers.

BOTTOM Tail of the US-spec bike, with a short rear mudguard, reflectors, and a lack of a seat strap and mirrors, the latter being optional in the States.

sampled." Others were impressed, too. *Cycle* even had a fold-out cover to make sure enthusiasts wouldn't miss out on the styling details, calling the Z1 "the most modern motorcycle in the world."

Magazines are one thing, of course, but ultimately punters vote with their wallets. Fortunately, Kawasaki's investment paid off. The success of the Kawasaki motorcycle division helped the company as a whole keep growing, with employment peaking at 34,771 in 1972 (over three times the figure from ten years earlier), and indeed remaining over the 30,000 mark until 1978. In America, too, the introduction of the 900 Z1 (demand outstripped supply for a long time) and the success of the regional sales structure brought KMC some record results, with a 50 per cent gain in sales and a huge increase in market share. The American arm of the company was set to expand its Stateside influence even further over the next few years.

BELOW The so-called 'general' specification Z1, which was basically the same as the North American model, but with rearview mirrors as standard. The headlight and indicators were the same as those used on the W-series, but the rear combination lamp was borrowed from the 1973-type S1A and S2A.

BELOW The first catalogue for the Japan-only Z2, or 750-RS, which was sold with just a single colour scheme. Careful inspection reveals a bike close to the 'general' specification, although amber rear reflectors were used, and the speedo should be calibrated up to 220kph with a heavy orange band starting at 80kph to be correct for the JDM Z2.

THE Z2

Nothing is ever easy, that's for sure. Here was Kawasaki with what looked like a surefire winner on its hands, and then an informal agreement made between the 'big four' during the Z1's development led to the 900cc machine being too big for the Japanese market – a 750cc limit was agreed upon, presumably to stop a displacement war before things got out of hand. It was probably a sensible move, but it did leave the folks in Akashi with something of a problem, and one that needed to be dealt with quickly.

Changing the cylinder bore would have been the simple answer, of course, but Inamura was far from happy with the test results, and duly changed both the bore and stroke to retain the four-pot unit's smooth performance and impeccable overall balance. A 64mm bore and 58mm stroke were chosen in the end, which – somewhat ironically – was the same relationship as that specified in the early days of the N600 project.

BELOW One of the few visual differences between the Z1 and Z2 ...

BELOW The rare Z2P police bike.

BOTTOM RIGHT Advert for Kawasaki helmets, featuring the Z2 shortly after its announcement. Sales of the domestic market's Z2 flagship model began in March 1973, with reports praising its superb response and handling.

When the Z2/KZ750A was announced to the press at the Tokyo Prince Hotel in December 1972, it quickly became obvious that the Z2 (sold from March 1973 as the 418,000 yen 750-RS in the showrooms) was for all intents and purposes a Z1 built for the home market, with a smaller 746cc engine to suit. With a 9.0:1 compression ratio and a bank of VM26SC carburettors, the Z2 delivered 69bhp at a heady 9000rpm, but other than some gearing and minor dimension revisions, there was little to tell the Z1 and Z2 apart. Indeed, even the colouring was the same, albeit limited to one hue on the Japan-only model.

BOTTOM One of the last W1 Special (W1SA) adverts from the January 1973 issue of *Autoby,* with the bike featuring a nine-fin head and optional pannier setup.

Z-series data register

A summary of early Z-series frame and engine start numbers, along with the main paint schemes used for each model according to Model Year release.

MY	Type	Frame No	Engine No	Colouring
1973	Z1	Z1F-00001 on	Z1E000001 on	Candy Brown with orange, Candy Green with yellow.
	Z2	Z2F-00001 on	Z2E000001 on	Candy Brown with orange.
1974	Z1A	Z1F-20001 on	Z1E020001 on	Candy Brown with orange, Candy Green with yellow.
	Z2A	Z2F-00001 on	Z2E000001 on	Candy Green with yellow.
1975	Z1B	Z1F-47500 on	Z1E047500 on	Candy Super Blue with gold, Candy Super Red with gold.
	Z2B	Z2F-00001 on	Z2E000001 on	Candy Super Blue with gold, Candy Super Red with gold.

Note: Unlike the Z1, Z2 frame and engine numbers were sequential rather than batched. The MY frame number splits were at approximately 03700 and 10350.

THE W3: LAST OF THE BREED

The W3, now officially sold under the 650-RS moniker to fall in with the Z2's 750-RS badging, was the last of the original W-series models, running alongside the W1SA for a little while before superceding it completely in response to the latest domestic emissions regulations. Many things were the same on the W3 and the late W1SA, but there were also many important differences that make it easy to distinguish the two models.

The first major deviation was the adoption of disc brakes up front – a double disc arrangement, as it happens, which was probably overkill given the bike's performance and weight, and ironically, the disc setup added a fair bit of bulk (16kg, or 35lb to be precise) into the equation that wasn't there before. While the wheel and tyre sizes were carried over, and the front mudguard was basically the same, the strengthening pieces on the latter were split, placed higher at the leading edge and lower at the trailing edge to give more clearance for the brakes.

An amber reflector was added to the lower part of the front fork, below the rubber bellows, while the area above it went back to being all-chrome. The indicators and headlight

were the same as the W1SA specification, although the gauges were changed again, from Nippon Seiki to Nippon Denso units with bullet-shaped tails, and a bank of four warning lights was set between them, just below the ignition barrel. There was another pair of warning lights in the tachometer face, and all came with wording to tell the rider of their function – a rule that found its origins in America, but it's often easier to comply on a global footing rather than

BELOW Catalogue for the W3. Pilot production started in September 1972, although sales did not officially begin until February 1, 1973. The W moniker was dropped at this stage, the company preferring to use the 650-RS name for the new model, thus creating an RS range for the big four-strokes to go with the established SS line of sporting two-stroke machines.

BOTTOM Studio shot of the 1973 Model Year W3 (650-RS). The twin used Dunlop K87 rubber at the rear, matched up with F6s at the front, incidentally, and production models featured a 200kph speedo and 10,000rpm tachometer, which is different to the catalogue illustration.

a localised one. On saying that, the speed warning light was not found elsewhere, and it's label was in Japanese!

Moving back, the tank badge was now chrome with a black background (it was the opposite on the W1SA), the tank itself painted black with heavy graphics in either Pearl Candy Ocean Blue or Pearl Candy Gold. Beyond that was a new dual seat with only a central pleat and belt to break it up. The oil tank and side box were much the same, finished in black, but the '650' logo strip trimming them was slightly different, with 'Roadster' wording added. The rear mudguard was carried over, as were the rear indicators, although the rear lamp usually had a single reflector on the W3s, despite the Mach models having the W1SA-spec lens. Beneath the mudguard, the wheel and tyre sizes were familiar to followers of W lore, but the rear drums were back to an all-silver finish, and the rear shocks were revised, being all-chrome, with more of the coil spring visible and with an amber reflector mounted close to the top in keeping

BELOW Japanese advertising from 1973 showing the RS range, which consisted of the 650cc W3 and 750cc Z2 roadsters.

with the 'safety equipment' line of development; other safety features included things like a kill switch and hazard warning lights.

The engine, with 'Daikon' exhausts, was not that much different to that of the late W1SA – a point strengthened by the fact that the last few W1 Specials actually had the same head as the W3, distinguished by having nine cooling fins rather than the ten found on earlier versions. These heads came with hardened valve seats and guides in preparation for unleaded fuel. Reduced lead content had been introduced in Japan in July 1971, but the spring of 1973 was to see the country go all the way and promote lead-free petrol. Most makers started making modifications long before 'Green Day', with Kawasaki amongst them. Other changes for the W3 included the adoption of the latest strict VM28 carbs, with a starter plunger not found on VM28SCs, but that was it – there was nothing else worthy of noting.

OTHER 1973 MY NEWS

The Americans finally got the 250 S1 in time for the 1973 season, priced at $815, although this is where some care is needed. For some strange reason, while the US market

BOTTOM The US line-up for the 1973 season, with prices initially ranging from $299 to $1895 (later in the year, the H1 had gone up to $1235, the H2 to $1499, and the Z1 to $1975, by which time the 441cc F12MX had joined the KMC range). For comparison, a look at the French catalogue for 1973 reveals the same Z1, H1 and H2 grades, older versions of the S1 and S2, the same F9, F11 and F6 scramblers, and a GA1-based '125 Touring' bike.

RIGHT One of the first S1s to arrive in America. It's not enough to say a 1973 model on the S for this season, as the old model was carried over in a number of markets. This, then, is the S1A, readily identified by the new tank stripes.

BELOW European catalogue for the 1973 Mach III (H1D). European bikes were equipped with Dunlop ribbed F3 tyres up front, K87s at the rear, and low handlebars. The model illustrated here has no reflectors, although some EU markets required them.

received the S1A with a narrow tank stripe and 28bhp, the Japanese plus a number of European and Australasian distributors kept going with the original S1 sporting its wavy rainbow coachlines and 4bhp more. Looking at the production figures probably explains things, as the 350 S2 was selling well, while the S1 was struggling to find its niche, even in Japan, where it should have been welcomed with open arms; by the end of 1972, only 11,141 S1s had been built, versus 41,664 S2s, and 1973 figures were only a few hundred units different on either side of 3600. Pricing policy probably didn't help, as the 350cc model was excellent value, and the 250cc grade couldn't have been sold for less given the manufacturing costs involved. A bigger gap between the two would make the smaller machine more attractive in due course.

Meanwhile, the 1973 S2 (or S2A to be totally correct) was released with the same colouring as the American S1A for most markets, although not all, as several European catalogues carried both the 1972 S1 and S2 models over into the 1973 season. Anyway, where it was sold, the S2A gained the same chrome mudguards, new seat, tail section, rear lamp and badging found on the 250cc S1A model, plus disc

brakes up front (something not fitted on the strict S2, even those sold in the 1973 MY), although power went down a fraction to 44bhp in order to meet emissions regulations.

Bigger changes were afoot for the H1D, or Mach III. The modified fuel tank shape and graphics was an obvious one, but the flip-up seat was also revised, and a new cowl was adopted beyond it, aping that found on the S1A and S2A, as well as the Z-series, of course. However, the old rear light unit was retained on the Mach III, so the top edge of

BELOW The 1973 S2A. While the strict S2 continued unchanged, the S2A (sold in America and parts of Europe) featured a number of styling revisions, including a new rear light off the Z1/Z2. The S2A also came with a cleaner engine and front disc brake not found on the S2, regardless of whether it was classed as a 1972 or 1973 model.

BELOW The 'general' specification H1D, similar to the US version in many respects, and seen here in the lime green livery that dominated advertising from the time. The H1 and both S-series models (at least in updated A guise) gained an inspection window on the oil tank for the 1973 season; it was added on the H2 for 1974.

the cowl was squared off to suit. The styling changes were rounded off by chrome mudguards, the removal of the air scoop on the rear brakes, new indicators that were brighter than before, repositioned reflectors (moving to the fork and three-position shocks when fitted), a new gauge pack, revised switchgear, and fresh badges on the oil tank and side box.

The exhaust pipes were tilted further up at the back, but they were also a touch quieter than the earlier set; the air cleaner assembly was revised to reduce noise at the same time as well, now being similar to the H2 design. Other modifications included new carb jets and needles bringing the VM28SC KA6 into play, and adopting an H2-type CDI ignition system, although this still couldn't stop buyers losing 1bhp and a little torque along the way. In addition, the shift linkage was revised, so it was no longer possible to make a bike with a right-hand gearchange, although the shift pattern itself was retained.

The engine was moved forward a fraction in a strengthened frame that was matched with an H2-type swing arm, which came with an additional bracing piece. With a 10mm (0.4in) longer wheelbase, weight increased to 185kg (407lb), but a lot of the extra bulk was to improve weight distribution to enhance handling and reduce the risk

RIGHT The mystery Candy Green H1D, which, according to the back of this flyer, sold for the same 320,000 yen as the Candy Lime version. Note the stripe on the tail section, as there's very little else to distinguish this from the H1E released for 1974.

BOTTOM European catalogue for the 1973 Mach IV (H2A).

of unwanted wheelies! The engineers were able to drop the steering damper as a result, offering it as an option instead for those that requested one.

One will remember the H1B and H1C causing us headaches in the previous chapter, well things were even harder to call with the second colour variation on the H1D. The first catalogues promoted the lime green shade to the point where one can be excused for assuming that was the only colour listed for 1973. But there was also a dark green model available, albeit late in Japan and America, that looked almost identical to the green version of the 1974 H1E. Earlier green H1Ds had the '500' badge rather than the one found on the H1E, but even this is not a surefire means of identification, as the later type badging with 'Mach III' underneath was adopted towards the end of the season, so the tail stripe is one of the few identifying features we can rely on, as this was dropped on the 1974 machines. All good fun, especially if you're trying to restore one ...

Thankfully, the H2 changes were less complex, with the 1973 H2A gaining a chrome front mudguard that was a touch longer than the earlier version, fresh colouring and graphics, a modified gauge pack, and new badges like those of the S-series (eventually adopted in Japan midway through the 1973 season). Revised carburettor jetting dropped power

RIGHT American advertising from the summer of 1973, with the H2 stealing the limelight, and the S1, S2 and H1 playing second fiddle.

BOTTOM RIGHT The rare purple H2A in Japanese trim. Note the early JDM badging.

BELOW The 'general' spec H2 for the 1973 season.

down from 74bhp to 71bhp, but that was still more than enough horses to keep even the most dedicated of speed freaks happy.

Kawasaki had 15 bikes listed for Japan in 1973, with four 90cc two-stroke variants (including the new G6/KE90A or 90TR two-stroke scrambler, followed by the G8T/KH90B, G8S/KC90A and MC1, badged respectively as the 90SS, 90DX and 90MS, from January), a pair of 125s (a new 125TR went on the line in April), three 250s, a couple of 350s, a single 500 and 650 grade, and a pair of 750s. Of those, the 250-SS was priced at 218,000 yen (20,000 yen less than the 350-SS), the 500-SS was 320,000 yen (with the lime green model selling from January, followed by the darker green version in the summer), and the 750-SS triple 365,000 yen, with purple colouring eventually reaching the JDM from the summer. As for the four-stroke big stuff, the 650-RS was 363,000 yen, while the 750-RS commanded 418,000 yen.

BELOW Kawasaki continued to develop its 99cc G7T and G7S lines for export only, mainly to Asian markets, and sold using the 'Tiger Power' slogan. Both were updated at the start of 1973, gaining new tank graphics and not much else thereafter. This is a 1975 MY G7T, the sports model, although the G7S looked similar, it just lacked an extra cog in the gearbox.

BELOW Alan Masek addressing the press and other guests at the official announcement of the Lincoln plant scheme, held at the Waldorf Astoria Hotel in New York in January 1974. Kiyoshi Yotsumoto and Yoji Hamawaki can be seen to his left, behind the H1E. Yotsumoto, KHI's long-serving President, moved into the Chairman's office in June 1977, allowing Zenji Umeda (a VP since mid-1975) to move up the ladder and take on the role of President; Umeda would ultimately keep that position until 1981. Meanwhile, Hamawaki and Masek departed from KMC in March 1978.

A US MANUFACTURING BASE

As well as having to deal with emission and noise regulations, there was another problem, too. America provided the Japanese with a huge outlet for its two- and four-wheeled machines (around two-thirds of the 240,000 bikes built by Kawasaki in 1973 found their way to US shores, for instance), but all makers were suffering from lower profit generation due to unfavourable exchange rates. For many years, the exchange rate between USD and JPY currency was fixed at 360 yen/$1, although President Richard Nixon abandoned the Bretton Woods System in 1971, and eventually a floating exchange rate system was introduced, changing everything. By the spring of 1973, the rate was around 260 yen per dollar, and although it slowly went in Japan's favour for a while after this, it hardly ever went above the 300 mark again. After the oil crisis and Nixon debacle, inflation followed in the States, combining with a severe fall in the value of the yen to make life even harder for Japanese exporters.

But Kawasaki (or Yoji 'George' Hamawaki to be precise, who was appointed President of KMC in March 1973 after many years of serving as VP) had a plan – a good one, too, that many other Japanese firms copied in the years that followed, and that was to build its products in America. This would save a fortune in shipping costs and import duties, reduce delivery times, and get around those unpredictable exchange rate fluctuations in a stroke.

After a great deal of research, the plan was approved by Kiyoshi Yotsumoto and the KHI hierarchy in August 1971, and an investment of $20,000,000 was put aside for the project. Land in Lincoln, Nebraska, was purchased in 1972, and the factory (later known as Kawasaki Motors Manufacturing Corporation, aka KMM, after it was separated from KMC in December 1981) duly opened for business in November 1974, with a capacity of 5000 units a month.

In the meantime, of course, Kawasaki and its compatriots had to deal with the first oil crisis of the seventies – easier said than done when you have to import every single drop of oil consumed from abroad. As well as the obvious pinch for road users, manufacturing was hit extremely hard, with shortages on a number of products holding up production, and a dire shortfall in orders. Combined with the exchange rate maladies, this double whammy would have hit the shipbuilding side the hardest, although a tanker boom thankfully kept things on an even keel so to speak. The respite didn't last long, however, and

RIGHT The KX250 was the first in a new line of pure MX machines, joined by the KX125 and KX450 in time for the 1974 Model Year. There was also the MC1M for enthusiasts on a budget, which also lacked road equipment in order to save weight.

BELOW RIGHT American advertising promoting the new 1974 line-up. The fabled 'Kawasaki Lets The Good Times Roll' punchline was adopted in time for the US 1974 season. Of the road rockets, the H1 commanded \$1455 and the H2 \$1825, while the Z1 was priced at \$2275.

the company was really hurting by 1975, ultimately grateful it had a factory in the States ...

The Lincoln plant was a trailblazing move, around five years ahead of Honda's first factory in the States (even though they'd been talking about it since 1972), and no less than a decade ahead of Toyota's first full-blooded US sortie. The 1975 season machinery built at the Lincoln site included the KZ400 from January 22, 1975 (albeit slowly at first, with engines shipped from Akashi) and the 'Jet Ski' leisure craft from July, with the 1976 Model Year KZ900A, KZ900LTD (aka the KZ900B) and Z1P following from August 1975, and the KE175 two months later.

As it happens, the Jet Ski was a lot more to Kawasaki than just a plaything, for a second R&D centre was established in 1974 at Shakopee in Minnesota concerned with the design and testing of engines and recreation vehicles outside the motorcycle field, leading to creations like the ATV (all-terrain vehicle) plus, amongst other things, new lines of snowmobiles and marine equipment.

THE 1974 MODEL YEAR

On the line since May 1973 (the month in which a record 20,000 units plus were built, although the 30,000 mark was broken thanks to the help of newly-introduced Kawasaki-made robotics only 14 months later), one of the most interesting 1974 models was the KX250 – a pure motocross machine that couldn't be used on the road. However, its chrome molybdenum frame and alloy rims showed that Kawasaki was serious about competing in the MX arena, a fact backed up by the 90cc MC1M released a few weeks later, and two more KXs that followed at the end of summer. There was more big news from Akashi, though. As well as tiddler updates and the usual season-by-season refresher programmes, the S3/KH400A went on the line in July 1973, and the four-stroke KZ400D was announced alongside it at the 1973 Tokyo Show. Having recently leaked to the press that the future lay in four-stroke machines, the KZ was hardly a surprise, but as an indicator of what was in store, the model was keenly awaited.

Anyway, the S3 (also known as the 400 Mach II or 400-SS) was basically an S2 with a larger 57mm bore to take the engine capacity up to 400cc dead. Power output was down to 42bhp, but the horses were delivered in a cleaner, more user-friendly manner (and a more refined manner, too, thanks to rubber mounts isolating the three-cylinder lump from the frame), and with more torque and revised gearing, the bike's performance still felt strong. This enabled the marketing folks to create a distance between the S1 and the newcomer that was hardly there with the S2. Now the buyer had a more clear-cut choice, with the pricing policy making it less tempting to simply ignore the 250cc model for the limited benefits it had given.

The 398cc KZ400 (aka the Z400, or 400-RS as it was known in Japan) was an air-cooled sohc twin featuring counter-rotating balancers on the crank (far from a new

BELOW European catalogue for the 400 Mach III, otherwise known as the S3. Described as an "ideal all-rounder," the 42bhp model was listed with red or blue paintwork for 1974; the smaller-engined S1 was sold in green only that year.

RIGHT The attractive KZ400 at the time of its debut.

BOTTOM RIGHT 1974 season line-up in a European catalogue, with all S, H and Z variants shown alongside each other for ease of reference.

idea, but rarely used at the time, despite the undoubted benefits in vibration reduction) and PCV, hooked up to a five-speed transmission. It was followed by the KZ400S with a drum up front rather than a disc brake, and was important in that it enhanced the four-stroke line in a useful manner, taking Kawasaki into a modern era.

With the S2 gone, the S1 (now with 28bhp in all markets) was brought into line with the new S3. Therefore, the 1974 S1B featured a revised fuel tank, seat and tail cowl design aping that of the 1973 Mach IIIs. Even the tank graphics were similar, although the round taillight

BELOW The 500cc H1E viewed from above, with a close-up of the gauge pack. Note the brake wear warning light at the base of the Nippon Seiki tachometer, and the blanking piece in the centre panel, where the speed warning light goes on JDM models.

BELOW Side view of the EU-spec 1974 Mach III in green. Note the badging on the side box and the lack of coachlines on the rear cowl.

was retained to give some differentiation between the S and H1; just to confuse everyone, the H2 adopted a round rear light for 1974, although the 750cc machine was distinctive enough in its own right, looking significantly heavier than its stablemates from a styling point of view. The S-series chrome front mudguard was standardized with the H1, too, with the new S3 having wider rubber at both ends compared to its S1 counterpart, as well as a front disc brake, which the S1 lacked, of course. Both S models had a strengthened frame with a longer wheelbase, by the way, increasing weight, but generally enhancing the overall riding experience.

The 1974 H1E, especially the green one, looked exactly like the late-1973 H1D, although the coachline was dropped on the tail, and mechanically, a new H1-only solid state CDI ignition system was adopted, along with the PCV vent. There was also the brake wear indicator adopted on all S, H and Z models for 1974 to provide another distinguishing feature.

The 1974 H2B was not sold in Japan, giving the Z2 (750-RS) a clearer run, although it was shipped abroad. With the oil crisis not yet biting, no expense was spared in bringing the bodywork up-to-date, with a new fuel tank, seat and restyled rear cowl to bring the Mach IV into line with the other triples. The fresh graphics were another way of bringing the four models closer together, with universal Mach badging on the sides, and the same indicators and reflector positioning, too, when fitted. Oddly, as we've already mentioned, the H2B gained a round rear lamp unit,

BELOW Tail of the 'general' specification 1974 Mach III, with the old rear light unit carried over, presumably to save costs, seeing as the later H1D was so similar.

BELOW The 1974 H1E illustrated in a European brochure.

although the Mach III one was still the old shape for 1974 for some reason. The oil level inspection window was also new for 1974 on the 750cc model, along with a fresh meter pack, with most of the warning lights moving to a centre panel. On the mechanical front, the H2B gained new exhaust pipes, a PCV vent, and revised carburettor jet settings, taking them back closer to the original specifications. Power stayed the same at 71bhp, although there was a fraction more torque released as a result of these changes. The steering damper was also modified, a new swing-arm added an inch (25mm) to the wheelbase in a bid to soften the handling, and an engine kill switch added.

As for the Z1, the 1974 Z1A gained a polished finish on the engine, and even though the main colours were carried over, this change and the redesigned graphics gave the bike a completely

BELOW The 1974 season European-spec H2B finished in brown.

RIGHT The green version of the 750cc H2B triple, viewed from the other side.

BOTTOM RIGHT Tail of the 'general' specification H2B Mach IV, with the revised rear lamp in plain view; earlier 750cc models had the same light unit as the Mach III.

different impression. Other than a brake wear warning light and a carburettor jetting change midway through the season, there was very little else to report regarding the flagship. It was the same story with the Z2A (750-RS), on the line from November 1973 but not going on sale in Japan until January 1974, although, despite having been discontinued on the Z1, the black engine finish was retained on this 465,000 yen model. As before, only one paintwork option was listed for the 750-RS, being the green shade for 1974.

The W3 (650-RS) was also given a mild face-lift for 1974, with the fuel tank gaining fresh Candy Dark Red or Candy Blue graphics, plus a number of other minor differences – modified switchgear and the use of a red reflector on the rear shocks rather than the original amber one being the main things, with the latter also a feature on the Z2A. The 415,000 yen W3 was manufactured until December 1974, by which time the Z2 had well and truly taken over the Kawasaki 'big bike' mantle, pushing the old-fashioned W-series into the shade somewhat. However, the W had provided a superb foundation on which to build, and refused to die lying down, as we shall see later on. In the meantime, even though none were built during 1975, the original W continued to be listed by Japanese dealers until the early part of spring 1976. It's ironic that it having taken so long to shift the last batch of these twins when they were new, beaten into submission by newer, more modern machines, they are extremely sought after in today's market.

Anyway, as one will have gathered from the W3 and Z2 prices, the cost of Kawasaki ownership had increased by quite some margin for the 1974 season – the additional manufacturing costs caused by the oil crisis simply couldn't be avoided, and had to be passed on to customers in order for the company to survive. By the spring of that year, domestic prices now started at 105,000 yen for the 90SS or 90MS, with the 250-SS commanding 250,000 yen, the 400-SS 300,000 yen, and the 500-SS a whopping 365,000

BELOW LEFT Riders on the storm. A 1974 Mach IV taking on the elements ...

BOTTOM LEFT & RIGHT The two colours available on the 1974 Z1, seen here on a pair of European-spec models.

BELOW RIGHT Selected pages from a European brochure for the Z1A, with its revised graphics. Actually, only the cover shot corresponds to strict European spec, with the other pictures showing a 'general' specification machine, as some continental markets required side markers.

CENTRE PR shot showing the European specification Z1A. Several were seen in the cult *Mad Max* film, but whether or not that was good publicity is open to question, of course ...

BELOW Tail of the 'general' specification Z1A, with a clear view of the tail graphics used for the 1974 season bikes.

yen – the same as the discontinued 750-SS had been literally only a couple of years earlier, and a far cry from the 1970 season price. The 400-RS joined the Japan line-up mid-season, listed at 298,000 yen.

TESTING TIMES

Sadly, circumstances saw to it that other interesting machines were destined to fall by the wayside alongside the struggling W-series, some even before they saw the light of day. Yamaha had tinkered with the Wankel rotary engine in 1972, and Suzuki actually managed to bring an RE-powered bike to market as a 1975 model. Kawasaki had also been playing with the rotary in the background, instigating project X99 in October 1972. Testing at Yatabe at the end of 1974 highlighted the RE's heavy fuel consumption, which basically signed the project's death warrant given that the prevailing sales environment was hardly kind to gas guzzlers. Ultimately, it was decided to drop the fascinating X99 project during the spring of 1975 – an inevitable conclusion given the times and the need for cutbacks. While 1974 was still a good year as far as motorcycle sales are concerned, especially in the early part of the season, 1975 saw Akashi's calendar year (CY) production numbers bomb in the wake of oil crisis woes, falling from 311,221 units to just 207,038.

BELOW Catalogue for the domestic market's Z2A.

BOTTOM The 1974 W3, or 650-RS.

The sparsity of all-new models and a scant advertising programme back up the observation on austerity measures, although a handful of bikes made it through in time for the 1975 MY, with the 100 G3T making its debut as an alternative to the G7T (largely sold in Europe rather than Asia), the KS175/KE175B becoming the new F7, the introduction of the KD125 and the KT250 trials machine, and a renewal of the KX400; the KD80 was another newcomer as 1975 proper began, although the next model to hit the lines at Akashi was probably of far greater interest ...

RIGHT Shots from the 1974 London Motorcycle Show, held at the start of the year. Note the Z1 award for the *MCN* (aka *Motorcycle News*) 'Machine Of The Year,' which the £1088 model won a record four years on the trot. Kawasaki UK (KMUK) was established on February 12, 1974, as it happens, followed by KMG in West Germany and KMA in Australia during 1975. In addition, KMC formed a subsidiary in Canada (CKM) in July 1974, making Kawasaki a truly global enterprise if one adds in its numerous CKD operations.

BELOW A couple of pieces of Japanese advertising – one from the early part of the 1974, and the other from late in the season, with the 400-RS augmenting the existing pair of RS grades.

Z-series timeline

A summary of major Z-series developments in the early days, putting things into chronological order. For leading specifications and production numbers, please refer to Appendix III.

- May 1972 – pilot production of the Z1/KZ900A begins at Akashi. Full production started in August that year, although the Z1 was built for export only with a minimum of 500 units per month scheduled. Introduced on the US market as a 1973 model at $1895.
- January 1973 – production of the Z2/KZ750A begins. Starting in March, sales of the 418,000 yen Z2 (badged as the 750-RS in brochures) are restricted to the Japanese market to provide the H2 triple (or 750-SS) with a sales niche.
- March 1973 – police versions of the Z1 and Z2 released (the Z1P and Z2P) on March 1, with California Highway Patrol being one of the first customers. Bike production at Akashi reached 1,000,000 units that month.
- 1976 MY – the Z1 is replaced by the KZ900 (KZ900-A4), and the Z2 by the KZ750 (KZ750-B1), with the latter duly sold in all markets. The Z900 and Z750 monikers are adopted for these models in certain countries.

5 END OF AN ERA

Bob Dylan had told us that the times were changing back in 1964, but even he couldn't have foreseen the upheaval of the seventies. The escalation of the Vietnam War, Watergate, and the global crisis following OPEC's decision to place an oil embargo on countries seen to be supporting Israel during the Yom Kippur War had far-reaching effects, with calls for reductions in air and noise pollution hitting manufacturers from a different angle.

LEFT English-language brochure for the 1975 range, with a Z1 and KZ400 on the cover. Note the lack of an S3, which was still being built, but in increasingly small numbers. From a peak of 13,743 units in 1974 CY, production of the 400cc triple dropped to 6404 units in the following year, and although 9623 were produced in 1976, the numbers were set to drop off dramatically thereafter.

The 1975 Model Year brought with it a wind of change, its effects not visible to the outside world until the 1976 season started. In amongst the numerous new and revised scrambler lines (the KD80, KD100, KD125, KD175, KM100, KX400 and KT250), there was a brand new KZ750B put on the production line in February 1975, although several were built ahead of this, including 27 in 1974. This was a four-stroke vertical twin, so the designation is perhaps a little strange continuing the Z2's code, implying that this five-speed 745cc dohc model (equipped with contra-rotating balance weights, like the KZ400) was classed as the big four's ultimate successor, when this was not actually the case.

Although the KZ750B wasn't sold until the start of the 1976 season in the States (being announced in August 1975), and even later in Japan, eventually reaching the domestic marketplace in April 1976 (badged as the Z750 Twin, which was often shortened to Z750T), its imminent introduction perhaps helps explain why so little was done to the Z2. Indeed, it's obvious that original thoughts pointed towards letting the Z2A run on unchanged, as the Z2B didn't go into production until the spring of 1975, with sales only beginning in June that year. As such, this is a rare beast, for its replacement – the Z750 Four (or Z750F) – had already made its Japanese debut

BELOW LEFT The 50bhp KZ750 Twin at the time of its US debut.

BELOW RIGHT Japanese advertising from the spring of 1975, with the Z2A still being illustrated, as the Z2B didn't go on sale until June that year, priced at 465,000 yen. However, the 1975 MY Z2A did inherit the same sealed chain newly fitted to the Z1B; thus allowing the chain oiler to be discontinued.

BOTTOM A couple of adverts from an Osaka dealer showing the 1975 Z2, a Z2A in standard guise from the early part of the year, and a Z2B fitted with various 'cafe racer' parts. Note the Z2B's upswept tail graphics. By the way, Dunstall was still working its tuning and customizing magic, modifying several Z1s.

by March 1976, having gone on the line in the New Year. Interestingly, the black engine finish was continued for the Z2B, as was even the old badging on the sides, although the new colouring was available, and in two shades rather than the traditional one for the late-1975 newcomer.

Thankfully things were a tad more straightforward on the Z1 and triples, with, by and large, typical MY revisions being introduced according to traditions established within each country. As it happens, America was particularly speedy in releasing its 1975 models. Starting at just $407, most of the line-up consisted of dual-purpose enduro and MX bikes, which was a sign of the times, although street machines dominated in the 400cc-and-over category.

The export-only Z1B was on the line in plenty of time for the 1975 season, featuring new colouring and graphics, larger side badges (the tail coachlines and the clear side numbering give an excellent quick recognition point), a few switchgear modifications, revised speedometer calibrations with tighter increments (from 20mph gaps in the marking down to 10mph on US and UK bikes, for example), and a new chain with sealed-in grease, allowing the chain oiler to be dropped from the 82bhp machine's spec sheet.

BELOW Beautiful publicity shots from the series used for the 1975 MY Z1 catalogue. Unfortunately, its printing lead-time meant that it failed to highlight the revised speedometer markings, so these pictures of the 'general' spec machine, combined with a few studio shots, are ultimately as useful as the full brochure.

BOTTOM RIGHT Tail of the 'general' spec Z1B. One can just about make out the new speedo markings with the aid of a magnifying glass.

The 1975 version of the 250cc S1 featured revised graphics (with a sharper design on the tank and a matching section on the tail cowl), the deletion of the 'Mach' badge on the sides, and a chrome strip added back to the base of the seat on export models to match the H-series (something dropped on S-series machines for 1974 when the S3 was launched). The S1C went on sale as a 1975 Model Year bike abroad, and was released on the home market within a couple of weeks of this, in November 1974, instead of Japan's usual January or spring launch date. For the record, as the season progressed, the S1C eventually inherited the fatter tyres found on the 400cc S3, although its replacement (badged as the KH250) was already on the line at Akashi by June 1975.

BELOW The European-specification Z1B for the 1975 Model Year, this example finished in the red shade, although it has to catch the light to reveal that hue. The Z1B was built until December 1975.

BELOW Candy Super Blue was the second colour option offered on the 1975 Z1s, although again, the light can play tricks on you. Both the blue and red paint shades were offered on the Z2B, too, incidentally.

BOTTOM LEFT A UK advert from the spring of 1975, including the Z1 road bike and the highly-successful Godier/Genoud racer.

BOTTOM RIGHT An Italian 1975 MY leaflet with the Z1B gracing the cover.

BELOW American advertising for the $2475 Z1B from November 1974. In a *Cycle World* three-way test against the BMW R90/6 and a Suzuki RE5, the Z1 came a tight second to the $3200 German twin. The magazine noted: "Kawasaki was very close with its first Z900. So close, in fact, that the present model shows few changes. Due to inflation, it's not quite the buy that it once was, but it still delivers everything the original did. And for that reason it remains one of the best buys in motorcycling."

As for the S3, the original version was sold in Japan minus 'Mach' badges to give the 400-RS more of the limelight, and indeed, the H2 was still not listed domestically for much the same reason, allowing the 750-RS (or Z2) some breathing space. An updated for 1975 S3A was built, however, featuring the same graphics and trim updates as the export S1C (JDM versions lacked the chrome seat strip to fit in with the old S3 being carried over) and not much else. Both S-series models had the same 28bhp and 42bhp power output as the previous season.

RIGHT A couple of pieces of Kawasaki's general advertising from the second half of 1975, one promoting rider safety, and the second featuring clothing and other gifts to be given away as presents to those responding to market research.

BELOW RIGHT Catalogue for the 1975 season S1C (Mach I) and S3A (Mach II). The S1 was offered in blue only, while the S3 came in red or green.

BELOW LEFT Tail of the European-spec H1 for 1975. This angle gives a clear view of the graphics added to the rear cowl for the 1975 season.

BOTTOM LEFT The 'general' specification H1F in Candy Brown.

The H1F was introduced as a 1975 model, and sold in Japan from November 1974. Again, there was nothing exciting about the update, just the colouring and markings on the 59bhp machine, and the same was true on the 71bhp H2C, too, apart from another 13mm (0.5in) extension on the wheelbase via a longer swing-arm; the wheelbase now stood at 1448mm (57.0in). This would be the last incarnation of the 208kg (458lb) Mach IV, as emissions and noise regulations saw to it that no-one was allowed to have fun anymore.

Selling at $1976 in the US ($457 more than the H1), *Cycle World* had this to say about the 750cc triple at the time: "The Z1 will [out-corner the H2 and also blow it] off at the drags without the ills of surging, vibration and poor gas mileage.

RIGHT Tail of the final H2 'Mach IV' model.

BELOW & BELOW RIGHT Catalogue for the 1975 season H-series models. The H1 was available in blue or brown, while the H2 was listed with red and purple colour options.

BOTTOM LEFT The European-spec 1975 Model Year H2C in red.

750 MACH IV H2

500 MACH III HI

SPECIFICATIONS

	H2	H1
PERFORMANCE		
Maximum horsepower	71 hp/6,800 rpm	59 hp/8,000 rpm
Maximum torque	7.9 kg-m/6,500 rpm (57.1 ft-lb/6,500 rpm)	5.7 kg-m/7,000 rpm (41.2 ft-lb/7,000 rpm)
Acceleration	SS 400 m (¼ mile): 12.0 sec.	SS 400 m (¼ mile): 12.4 sec.
Minimum turning radius	2.4 m (94.5 in.)	2.3 m (90 in.)
Fuel consumption	30 km/l @ 48 kph (85 mile/Imp. gal. @ 30 mph)	33 km/l @ 50 kph (95 mile/Imp. gal. @ 30 mph)
Braking distance	12 m @ 50 kph (40 ft @ 31 mph)	10.5m @ 50kph (35ft @ 31mph)
ENGINE		
Type	2-stroke, 3-cylinder, piston valve	2-stroke, 3-cylinder, piston valve
Displacement	748 cc (45.63 cu. in.)	498 cc (30.4 cu. in.)
Bore and stroke	71 × 63 mm (2.795 × 2.48 in.)	60.0 × 58.8 mm (2.36 × 2.31 in.)
Compression ratio	7.0 : 1	6.8 : 1
Ignition system	Electronic CDI	Electronic CDI
Starting system	Kick	Kick
Lubrication	Injectolube (Oil injection)	Injectolube (Oil injection)
Engine oil	2-stroke oil	2-stroke oil
TRANSMISSION		
Type	5-speed, constant mesh, return shift	5-speed, constant mesh, return shift
Shift pattern	N-1-2-3-4-5	N-1-2-3-4-5
Clutch	Wet, multi-disc	Wet, multi-disc
FRAME		
Type	Tubular, double cradle	Tubular, double cradle
Suspension: Front	Telescopic fork	Telescopic fork
Rear	Swing arm	Swing arm
Tyre size: Front	3.25 – 19 4PR	3.25 – 19 4PR
Rear	4.00 – 18 4PR	4.00 – 18 4PR
DIMENSIONS		
Length, overall	2,175 mm (85.6 in.)	2,125 mm (83.7 in.)
Width, overall	831 mm (32.7 in.)	825 mm (32.5 in.)
Height, overall	1,180 mm (46.5 in.)	1,100 mm (43.3 in.)
Wheelbase	1,448 mm (57.0 in.)	1,410 mm (55.5 in.)
Ground clearance	139 mm (5.5 in.)	145 mm (5.7 in.)
Dry weight	208 kg (459 lbs.)	185 kg (407 lbs.)
Fuel tank capacity	17 litres (3.7 Imp. gal.)	16 litres (3.5 Imp. gal.)
Oil tank capacity	2 litres (1.8 Imp. qt.)	2.3 litres (2.0 Imp. qt.)

Specifications subject to change without notice.

KAWASAKI
HEAVY INDUSTRIES, LTD.
ENGINE AND MOTORCYCLE GROUP

99960-012-19 Printed in Japan

BELOW Japanese flyer from the tail-end of 1975, before the 1976 MY changes were introduced, which was January 1976 for the domestic market in a lot of cases. The range was actually much the same as it was at the end of 1974, with only the 250TX trials bike (aka the KT250) added in the spring of 1975, and the brand new KM90 taking the place of the 90MS for 1976, but otherwise carried over, even down to pricing. As such, with prices starting at 109,000 yen, the 250-SS cost 250,000 yen, the 400-SS 300,000 yen, the 500-SS 365,000 yen, the 400-RS 298,000 yen, the 650-RS 415,000 yen, and the flagship 750-RS 465,000 yen.

“The king of superbikes is simply no longer king. Worse yet, its very existence is threatened by a sometimes unrealistic EPA and government preoccupation with noise. Time has dictated that a change is due. Perhaps overdue. And in a way that’s sad, because brute power machines like the H2 turned a lot of people on at a time when all of us could afford to be carefree.”

BELOW This American advert for Lester alloy wheels actually dates from 1976, but it shows a 1975 Z1. Alloy rims were becoming more and more popular for bikes at this time.

Competition review: 1972 onward

Giacomo Agostini was again untouchable in the 1972 FIM championship, taking all but two races in the 500cc category. As was the case in 1971, Dave Simmonds was Kawasaki’s top finisher in both the 125cc and 500cc standings, although a second in Spain was his best performance with the H1 that year. Sadly, Simmonds was destined to die young in a freak off-track accident a few weeks later, in October 1972. His rise to the top against the odds would make an excellent movie one day!

In America, Bob Hansen was in charge of the semi-works effort for 1972, signing Yvon Duhamel, Gary Nixon and Paul Smart to ride the fresh-out-of-the-box H2-Rs supplied by the factory (only ten were built in 1972) for his new team. As Dan Hunt of *Cycle World* noted in his pre-season ramble: "Assuming that the new 750s are reliable (we already know that they are fast), I pick Kawasaki to give the most consistent results in the AMA road race nationals. As a team, they will score the greatest number of points."

One of the first H2-R racers at the Akashi works.

Indeed, the H2 seemed ideally suited to the ACU and AMA Formula 750 rules, with the American race series having particular appeal for the Japanese maker. Daytona did not go to plan, though. Duhamel charged as usual, but his H2 gave up, Nixon dropped out with a gearbox problem, and Smart failed to even get off the line. The only consolation was that the Suzukis and Hondas faired no better, and the Yamaha that won was a private entry! The top Kawasaki was 27th, so it was back to the drawing board ...

Thankfully, things picked up at Road Atlanta, with Duhamel first, Smart second and Nixon fifth, behind a Triumph and a BSA, but there was more disappointment at Loudon and Laguna Seca. At least Talledega was kinder, with the three Team Hansen bikes in the money – first, second and fourth, with Smart then claiming his first victory of the year at Ontario. Although the pre-season prediction wasn't quite right, the potential was there.

The FIM approved a race series for 750s outside the world championship during the spring of 1972, in readiness for the 1973 season, which is when the FIM and AMA started working together. This still left Kawasaki in something of a bind, for the FIM's restriction on the number of cylinders allowable ruled out S1 and S2 production racers for the 250cc and 350cc classes (there was, however, a one-make series called the Coupe Kawasaki in France using the 350 S2 Mach II models). Interestingly, Kawasaki started taking motocross more seriously instead, with the purposeful F11M of 1972 being a case in point. At least the H1-R kept battling away (115 were built in the end), and in March 1973, the H2-R was at last released for sale to the public.

The Kawasaki team at Daytona in 1973. From left to right: Hurley Wilvert, Masahiro Wada, Art Baumann, Cliff Carr, Yvon Duhamel, and Gary Nixon.

The 1974 water-cooled H1-RW, of the type Mick Grant won the Senior 500cc TT race with.

The 100bhp H2-R had a wide power band, making it a lot more user-friendly than traditional two-stroke racing machinery. Dual discs up front helped pull the bike down from 175mph (280kph) with an element of safety; with the H2-R weighing only 145kg (319lb), they were well up to the job. According to factory figures, though, only three were built in 1973, and another in 1974 giving a total run of just 14 bikes. This was a real rarity!

The water-cooled KR750 of 1975, based on the H2-R.

The H1-R was basically outclassed in the FIM series, and things didn't improve a great deal in the 1973 AMA races either, at least not initially, with Art Baumann eighth at Daytona behind a gaggle of Yamahas; Yvon Duhamel was ninth. After that, with magnesium alloy wheels and fresh disc brakes, Kawasaki's luck changed for the better: Gary Nixon won at Loudon, and again at Laguna Seca, followed home by Cliff Carr, then made it a hat-trick at Pocono. Ontario saw Kawasaki score a one-two-three (Duhamel first, Nixon second, Baumann third), which was enough to secure Nixon the championship title.

A nice piece of Akai publicity material from the tail-end of 1979.

The 1972 'Project 0280' prototype powered by a square-four. Although a rarity in the modern era, there have been a number of excellent square-fours in the past, with Edward Turner's Ariel 4F springing to mind as a perfect example.

Kawasaki kept a relatively low profile in 1974, cutting the race budget by a huge amount, partly in response to the fuel crisis, which hit the Japanese maker particularly hard due to its reliance on heavy industry and petrol engines, and partly due to fresh commitment to the MX side of the competition spectrum that ate a fair chunk of what was left in the pot. Hurley Wilvert was third at Daytona (reduced to 180 miles), but it was a bad year in AMA racing, and only the Frenchman Christian Leon seemed to be keeping the green and white flag flying in FIM circles; he finished the season in 20th. Even the Formula 750 series was failing to provide rewards, with Barry Sheene winning for Suzuki in the first year (1973), and John Dodds of Yamaha claiming second. In fact, Yamaha would win the F750 crown from 1974 to 1979.

In the background, Kawasaki managed to develop an 85bhp water-cooled version of the H1-R called the H1-RW. Only a handful were built, and while it failed to shine at Daytona, it has a real claim to fame, allowing Mick Grant to win the big race at the 1975 Isle of Man TT. Grant would be a name one readily associates with the Kawasaki marque, especially after the UK-based Team Kawasaki, ably ran by Stan Shenton, started winning with the new water-cooled two-stroke KR-series.

The KR750 triple was an evolution of the H2-R, coming with a fresh 68mm x 68mm bore and stroke to give 741cc, plus a six-speed transmission. Pumping out 120bhp at 10,000rpm, the crank was a little over-stressed on the early 1975 engines, adding to teething troubles, although it took Gary Nixon to second in the 1976 Daytona 200, Kawasaki to second overall in the F750 title chase from 1976 to 1979, and Mick Grant won the Classic 1000cc TT race at the Isle of Man on one in 1977 and 1978. His average speed was 110.8mph (177.3kph) en route to his 1977 victory, the fastest of the entire meeting (the first in which the legendary TT was dropped from the championship calendar due to safety concerns), creeping up to 112.4mph (179.8kph) in the following year, complete with a remarkable fastest lap of 114.3mph (182.9kph) along the way.

The KR250 and KR350 (both introduced in time for the 1975 racing season) were unusual, being inline 'tandem' twins, with one cylinder ahead of the other, as opposed to the traditional layout for a twin, as found in the Kawasaki W-series. These water-cooled two-stroke models employed rotary disc valve induction matched with Mikuni carburettors, although the engine construction underwent several changes over the years, as did the suspension, with late models employing a 'Uni-Trak' shock absorber setup at the back. By 1977, the 250cc model was showing signs of things to come, and Kork Ballington was declared both 250cc and 350cc world champion in 1978 and 1979 using KR power. Works rider Anton Mang kept up the momentum with a 250cc title in 1980 (plus second in the 350cc category), both crowns in 1981, and the reverse of the 1980 situation in 1982.

The four-cylinder KR500 being put through its paces at the JARI test site in Tsukuba by Akihiko Kiyohara, Kawasaki's test rider who also raced.

The final part of the KR jigsaw was the KR500. Kawasaki had been weighing up the possibility of creating a two-stroke 750cc square-four road bike since the start of 1972. Several prototypes were made, but the project was scrapped in the summer of 1973 due to exhaust emission concerns. It was, however, the inspiration behind the KR500 GP racer.

The water-cooled KR500 had a 495cc four (basically a pair of KR250 units giving around 120bhp) mounted at an angle within an aluminium monocoque frame, hooked up to a six-transmission. While the KR250 and KR350 had given some excellent results, the KR500 sadly never lived up to expectations. Perhaps with this in mind, Kawasaki announced it was withdrawing from Grand Prix racing at the end of 1982, bringing an exciting era to a close. That isn't the end of the story, of course, for the Z1 was pretty handy at the track.

Although it won on its debut outing in a US production road race, the first 'competition victory' of note for the Z1 was the breaking of the 24-hour speed record at Daytona Speedway in mid-March 1973 during a KMC-backed publicity stunt. Equipped with drop handlebars and ridden by racers

Atmospheric shot from the speed record breaking session at Daytona, March 13-15, 1973, with Cliff Carr (left) and Bryon Farnsworth seated on the two bikes used for the 24-hour stint. The bike Duhamel used for the outright speed run had a fairing over the front.

Kawasaki advertising making the most of the Godier/Genoud partnership, produced in numerous European languages. They won two of the four Coupe FIM D'Endurance rounds in 1974, plus other events outside the championship. Honda dominated the series for a few years in the late-seventies before a Kawasaki comeback in 1981.

Baumann, Wilvert, Nixon, Carr, Wada, KMC man Bryon Farnsworth (who was involved with the Z1 from the prototype stages), plus journalists Cook Neilson and John Weed, two Z1s were ran around the clock to set a new 24-hour record of 2630 miles (4208km) and 109.6mph (175.4kph) despite some testing conditions caused by morning fog. At the same session, amongst other achievements (a remarkable 52 records were said to have been broken), Yvon Duhamel set an outright speed record on a third Yoshimura Racing-prepared Z1, clocking a staggering 160.2mph (256.3kph). If you can find the video, you'll see that this 106bhp machine sounded absolutely magnificent with its four-into-one exhaust system!

As it happens, David Aldana won the Heavyweight Production category at Daytona in 1975, riding a Hideo 'Pops' Yoshimura-prepared Z1, while Yvon Duhamel had a good level of success on a similar machine. Kawasaki also took an active role in the AMA Superbike Series, inaugurated in the following year. Reg Pridmore actually won the Superbike title for Kawasaki in 1977 and 1978 with the Z1000, and more silverware would follow for the Japanese maker in due course. As a matter of interest, Duhamel's son, Miguel, would go on to be an AMA champion in the 1990s, albeit with Honda.

Meanwhile, back in Europe, the FIM Endurance Cup (renamed the European Championship in 1976 before gaining world championship status in 1980) was made up of a series of long-distance races, with the French classic Bol D'Or bash being the jewel in the crown. Georges Godier and Alain Genoud won this prestigious event in both 1974 and 1975 with a Z1, the latter being a clean sweep of the podium for Kawasaki as it happens, but a six-lap winning margin – not to mention beating Duhamel – proved the French pair's credentials beyond doubt. Godier and Genoud would go on to win several big endurance races in the mid-seventies, later creating a special Z1-based machine in conjunction with designers from Amiens University. By this time, they themselves had retired, and concentrated on race management instead – it would be up to other exponents to keep the Kawasaki flag flying over Europe, and there was no shortage of those ...

AN UNSURE FUTURE

The company was faced with one problem after another in the mid-seventies. The effects of the first oil crisis hit everyone, with even American car manufacturers giving up their 'Yank Tank' mentally and downsizing – a move that was even more discernible as the second oil crisis took its toll. With Japan recovering slowly, due to its oil dependence and distinct lack of the black stuff in its own backyard, Kawasaki was in the same boat, being forced into rethinking future policy due to outside circumstances beyond its control. Bikes would become more and more focused on target user groups as time went on.

In America, sales were down generally 44 per cent in 1975 compared to two years earlier, and although KMC had managed to buck the trend in 1974 (and even overtook Yamaha in the sales league in the following season, putting Kawasaki second behind Honda, at least for a little while, as the Akashi firm outsold Suzuki in the US for the first time at the end of 1973), the new Lincoln facility naturally absorbed huge amounts of money as a large enterprise start-up. Thankfully, it would quickly come good, but short-term, it was another financial headache to deal with, well up there with the significant increase in manufacturing costs.

Exchange rates were unhelpful on Japan-built exports, being around 300 yen to the dollar at the end of 1975 but set to drop dramatically (a sustained nosedive saw the yen trading at 180 three years down the line), and emissions concerns were still in the background, too. Indeed, in February 1976, a decision was made to make all bikes with an engine capacity exceeding 125cc as four-stroke models. There was another problem distinctly unique to Japan, and that was the increasing trouble the country was having with youthful bike gangs, called bosozoku. This made the government make it significantly harder to get a licence for 750cc machines from late-1975 onwards, which undoubtedly hurt the Akashi firm.

Things could have been worse, of course. The end of the British motorcycle industry was nigh, and America had only Harley and – somewhat ironically – Kawasaki still in the game.

The replacements

This table gives a brief summary of the models that replaced the existing H and Z lines for the 1976 season, along with what was the S-series triples to help put things into perspective. The Mach IV (H2) was not replaced, of course.

Previously	Type	Notes
Mach I (S1)	KH250	Built in Akashi only. Continuation of S1 frame and engine numbers. Paint in Candy Super Red or Candy Sky Blue, then Metallic Deep Red. KH250A has drum brakes up front, KH250B has disc brakes.
Mach II (S3)	KH400	Built in Akashi only. Continuation of S3 frame and engine numbers. Paint in Metallic Dark Green or Metallic Deep Orange.
Mach III (H1)	KH500	Built in Akashi only. Continuation of H1 frame and engine numbers. Paint in Metallic Burgundy Red or Metallic Copper Brown.
Z1	KZ900	Built in Lincoln from August 1975 (with frame numbers starting on 500001, but a continuation of older engine numbers), and Akashi from December (continuing original Z1 frame and engine numbers). Paint in Diamond Brown or Diamond Dark Green.
	KZ900LTD	Limited KZ900B model built in Lincoln, and later, from January 1976, in Akashi, too. Frame numbers included within KZ900A runs. Paint in Classic Red.
Z2 (750-RS)	KZ750F	Built in Akashi only, from January 1976. Direct Z2 replacement with four-cylinder engine. Continuation of Z2 frame and engine numbers. Paint in Diamond Green or Diamond Brown.
	KZ750T	Built in Akashi only. Indirect H2 replacement with two-cylinder engine. Unique 'KZ750B' frame and engine numbers. Paint in Diamond Red.

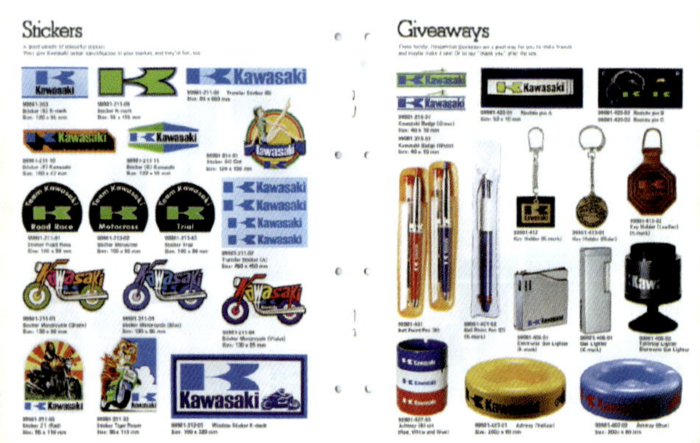

LEFT A couple of pages from the 1976 sales promotion brochure. Other items included a range of leaflets, films, posters, clothing and showroom goods.

BELOW LEFT Cute brochure from Kawasaki's Italian distributors.

NOT QUITE THE END

The 1976 Model Year signalled the end of a glorious era, as well as the start of a new one, naturally. The W had basically gone, with only a few hanging around as NOS, the H2 Mach IV had gone once and for all, and the Z-series and remaining triples were all reborn with new monikers fitting in with a general naming theme of KH representing the two-stroke road bikes and KZ the four-stroke machines. Therefore, as far as the author is concerned, this is the end of our story. But not quite, of course ...

In reality, the S1's replacement was much the same as its predecessor, with a typical makeover for the new season, including graphics and badging changes, plus a fresh seat and rear cowl design. The 250cc triple still pumped out 28bhp in most markets for 1976, although a few had a cleaner 26bhp engine installed. One of the biggest differences

THIS PAGE Useful catalogue showing the three remaining triples, with a 500cc model on the cover, and the disc-braked version of the 250cc machine inside.

was the availability of a front disc brake setup, with this version known as the KH250-B1; the drum-braked model was given the KH250-A5 designation. For the record, the latter was the norm in America, while Japan had the B1 model, introduced on the home market in January 1976.

The KH250, having gained disc front brakes for all markets for the 1977 season, limped on worldwide into the 1980 Model Year, by which time it looked very modern, thanks to some rather clever graphics and colouring. However, after averaging around 7000 sales a year for some time, it suddenly disappeared from showrooms with a complete lack of ceremony.

The KH400-A3 was announced in Japan and elsewhere at the same time as the new KH250, and featured the same styling changes. Sadly, despite a revised CDI ignition based on the type used by Kawasaki's off-roaders, power dropped to 38bhp at 7000rpm, and even 36bhp in some places. Exports of the KH400 ended with the 1978 model, although Japan kept it alive well into the 1980 season, with the same livery as the KH250.

With the H2 no longer with us, the KH500-A8 became the flagship of the triples line-up, but that couldn't stop a loss of power – down from 59bhp to 52bhp at 7000rpm, or a level 50bhp in certain markets. Introduced in Japan later than elsewhere, in April 1976, it featured the same set of styling changes as the KH250 and KH400, a revised 'one down, four up' shift pattern to match the other KH pair, a brighter headlight from the KZ900, and a larger rear brake drum. Amazingly, in spite of these updates, that was the last anyone heard of the KH500. Including H1s, 4903 of the 500cc triples had been built in 1975, but only 1768 made it off the line in the 1976 CY, bringing a wonderful era to a close.

As for the Z1, the 1976 model was called the KZ900 or Z900 rather than the Z1, and officially classed as the KZ900-A4. This implies it was a continuation of the

BELOW One of a series of shots taken for the Australian 1976 MY catalogue, showing the contemporary Z900 (left) and the Z400. Some markets filled the gap with the Z750 twin, and/or the Z650.

BOTTOM American advertising from the spring of 1976, and showing the $2475 KZ900. According to the factory, 10,000 900cc models were built at Akashi during 1976, and a further 6200 were produced at the Lincoln plant, including LTDs.

BELOW The Diamond Brown version of the 1976 Z900: this example being for the European market.

series, nonetheless, and indeed, at first glance it does look much the same as its predecessor. There was new badging, colouring and graphics, naturally, but also a revised reflector arrangement and a square rear light unit, not to mention dual discs up front as standard. As well as a change in the carburation (with smaller Mikuni VM26SSs now used, knocking just 1bhp off the maximum power output, and 1lbft from the peak torque figure), there were some minor changes to the gauges, too, plus an audible turn signal warning to improve safety.

The interesting thing was that the KZ900-A4 was also built at the Kawasaki plant in Lincoln, America – a few months ahead of it going on the line at Akashi, in fact. This gave rise to a short-run LTD model (the KZ900B), with a special US-sourced seat and four-into-two exhaust system, and fat Goodyear tyres mounted on cast alloy wheels, as well as Z1Ps built for the US police. While the Lincoln-built Z1P was unique to the States, duly featuring in the hit TV

BELOW Advertising from the spring of 1976 for the JDM Z750 Four, priced at 485,000 yen. By this time, the Japanese line-up had been completely revamped, featuring the KC90, KE90, KM90, KC125, KE125, KX125, KH250, KX250, KH400, Z400, KH500, Z750T and Z750F. The 90SS, 125MX, 250TR, 250TX and 650RS were hanging on when the new 750s made their debut, but only until stocks ran out; the 250TX became the KT250, by the way.

show *CHiPs*, based in Los Angeles, the LTD was eventually made in Akashi, too. However, the KZ900 and KV900LTD pairing were destined to fall by the wayside in all markets at the end of the 1976 season, moving over for a new 1000cc series.

We mentioned the Z2 changes at the start of the chapter, with the Z750 Four (or Z750F) taking its place in the line-up in the spring of 1976. I don't think anyone would argue that this was a Z2, as even the distinctive black finish on the engine was carried over, although the graphics and badging were brought up-to-date, matching those of the other 1976 MY KZ range. Closer inspection reveals a double disc setup at the front, the loss of the side reflectors, and the adoption of a square rear lamp. This new spec added 4kg (9lb) to the bike's weight, which was an acceptable amount given the added safety element twin discs bring. Interestingly,

BELOW The US 1976 Model Year line-up, including a full line of triples, the KZ750 twin augmenting the KZ400 and KZ900, and the KZ900LTD. The Americans were set to get some interesting new machines for the 1977 season.

despite the same carburettors and compression ratio, engine power increased a fraction to 70bhp at 9000rpm, while maximum torque output dropped to 40lbft at a heady 8500rpm.

The Z2 had been for domestic consumption, of course, and the same is true of the Z750F. However, several export markets were given the new 745cc (78mm x 78mm) twin – the 55bhp KZ750B – for the 1976 season, as this filled the gap left by the loss of the H2. Oddly, this 218kg (480lb) machine was also sold in Japan alongside the Z750 Four, being called the Z750 Twin (or Z750T) to distance it from its JDM stablemate.

The original Z750F (part of the same KZ750A series as the Z2) was built until 1977 (with around 3000 units produced), with the KZ750D taking its place, albeit still badged as a Z750 Four in the catalogues; unlike the KZ750A, this one was exported. Meanwhile, the KZ750B-type Z750T continued to be built until the end of 1978 ...

While all this was happening, there was the end of another era, with Kiyoshi Yotsumoto moving into the Chairman's office in June 1977, making way for a new, younger management team. With Zenji Umeda named as President, a number of company departments were

BELOW Viewing the KZ750B (or Z750T) from this angle shows the two-cylinder engine off nicely ...

BELOW An Australian brochure showing the new Z1000 and Z650 models. The existing KH100 was joined by a KH125 two-stroke single and Z200 four-stroke single for 1977, filling out the other end of the range.

streamlined in order to cut overheads and speed up the numerous processes that make things tick along. It was interesting to note that a larger R&D budget was being secured, too, so the cost reductions were certainly being put to good use.

A NEW GENERATION

It's all very well dwelling on the past, but one has to look forward as well, and, with the benefit of hindsight, Kawasaki's future certainly looked bright. As a 'big bike' book, covering the origins of what would quickly become a legendary marque, we cannot leave things here without a brief look at the products that bridge the gap between the main subject in this volume and the story to come in our next Kawasaki tome on the Ninja series. In reality, some still class the early KZs as Z-series models, so a few words certainly won't go amiss.

Two key four-stroke, four-cylinder products went on the line at Akashi in December 1975, although both would have to wait until the 1977 season to hit the showrooms. The first was the 83bhp replacement for the KZ900A – the dohc 1015cc (70mm x 66mm) KZ1000A, while the other was the 652cc (62mm x 54mm) KZ650B, a 64bhp spiritual

LEFT HRH Prince Charles trying one of the first Z1000s for size.

successor to the W-series in effect; both came with twin-cams, a four-into-two exhaust system, and a five-speed transmission with a traditional chain drive.

It's the KZ1000 (or Z1000 in some markets) that holds the most interest, though. Looking much like the KZ900, but with disc brakes at both ends, 21 were built in Akashi

BELOW American advertising for the 1977 Model Year Z1000.

BELOW The LTD featured in an American catalogue.

BELOW A Z1-R on test at the Akashi factory in June 1977. The 1978 MY machine had gone on the line there in May, and was offered with two fuel tank options to suit the owner – a larger one for touring, and a smaller one for keeping weight to a minimum.

in 1975, rising to almost 24,000 units in the following year. In addition, 13,392 were produced at the Lincoln plant in 1976, including a handful of 85bhp KZ1000LTD models, similar in style to the earlier 900cc version. For the record, the LTD (KZ1000B) was also made at Akashi from October 1976 onwards.

With production at Akashi having passed the two-million mark in early 1977, the KZ1000A was given a very mild face-lift for the 1978 season, by which time the KZ1000D (better known by the Z1-R moniker) had reached the showrooms. This 90bhp export-only machine featured the latest straight-edge styling that signalled the end of the 'classic' era once and for all. Although the front fairing was unique to the Z1-R line, the boxy fuel tank and rear cowling was to become a signature on the new Kawasakis, with the 1979 KZ1000-A3 following this lead to create the 'Z1000 Mk II' model.

By this time, for the 1979 season, Kawasaki was fielding the Z1300, as well as a shaft-drive version of the Z1000, called the Z1000ST. The top-end of the range continued to be developed, with 1100cc models augmenting the line-up, and there was even a turbocharged 750 added in 1983. But it was December 1983 that will be remembered, for that is when the press launch of the GPz900R took place. Known universally as the Ninja, the water-cooled four-cylinder ZX900A started a new chapter in the history books. Fittingly, it will start a new volume in our own series on Kawasaki motorcycles ...

BELOW There was certainly no shortage of glamour attached to the Z1-R – Kawasaki's interpretation of the iconic cafe racer, and a classic name revived into the bargain.

RIGHT What the Kawasaki range looked like for the 1980 season in Europe.

OPPOSITE One of the styling mock-ups for the Ninja ...

A W-series revival

Japan seems to go through a fairly regular cycle of retro booms, and motor manufacturers have always been quick to respond to the whims of fashion-conscious enthusiasts. The Nissan POA made its debut at the 1987 Tokyo Show, for instance, followed by the Figaro, and makers have been offering factory styling mods for years to give home market cars a vintage look. Mitsuoka products are another example of the Japanese obsession with a bygone era, albeit in conjunction with modern reliability.

On the bike side, while some will cite the Zephyr of 1989 as a 'retro' model, it all depends on when you were born – it still looks modern to the author! It was a great success in terms of sales, though, encouraging Kawasaki to go the extra mile and introduce a true modern oldie in the shape of the Estrella. Powered by an air-cooled 249cc single, this attractive machine has continued in production for over a quarter of a century. The 'Final Edition' of 2017 featured

When project 422 was first put on the drawing board, literally dozens of sketches were made, not only covering the general styling and individual components, but engine detailing as well. Ultimately, Kawasaki knew that a machine like this had to look right, not just feel right on the road. For engineering fans, the W650 would be as much an objet d'art as a motorcycle.

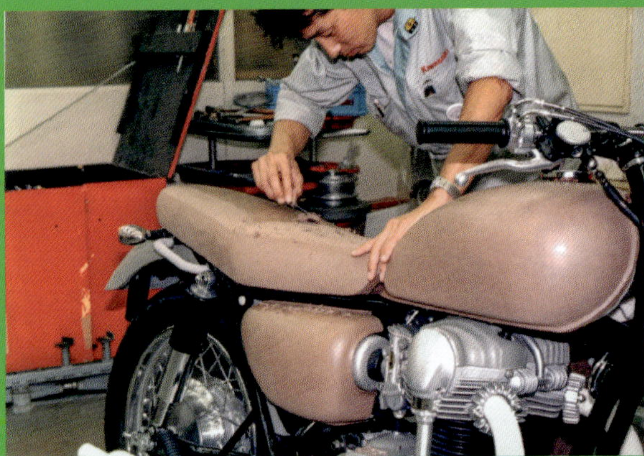

A W650 styling mock-up being crafted in the Kawasaki workshops.

One of the W650 prototypes, pictured here in October 1997.

W3 colouring, which was a novel link with the past.

The Z650/4 had actually been extremely popular in its time, and this observation, linked with the phenomenal success of the Estrella, was undoubtedly the reason Kawasaki brought out the 1999 W650. This 686,000 yen machine employed a four-stroke 675cc (72mm x 83mm) air-cooled vertical-twin, which gave 50bhp in a clean and reliable fashion. Different colouring and numerous limited editions were offered thereafter, with a 399cc variant sold between 2006 and 2009 to take advantage of local licensing rules.

Catalogue for the 1999 W650, which was available in two colours.

The W650 was duly followed by the W800, powered by a 773cc engine (the extra displacement being achieved by boring out the old block to 77mm) that delivered 48bhp. Launched in 2011, fuel-injection saw to it that emission codes were cleared with ease. In its last incarnation, announced in mid-2016, the 925,000 yen 'Final Edition' model was given a Candy Sunstone Charcoal and orange paint scheme, and was still being listed by Japanese dealers at the time of writing, in summer 2018. The author is busy saving up for one ...

The 2006 W400, this one in red, with black as the other option that year. The 29bhp machine was often customized, with numerous parts available from dealers.

The W800 at the time of its debut.

The W800 'Final Edition' is a handsome machine, readily evoking memories of the W3. Something new to replace it is hopefully in the pipeline.

APPENDIX I

CLASSIC W-SERIES SPECIFICATIONS & PRODUCTION FIGURES

SPECIFICATIONS

Specifications relate to the original version of each grade, although most continued with the same specs throughout their production life. Any mid-run changes are noted within the text.

650 W1 (export version) leading specifications

Engine type	Air-cooled four-stroke vertical-twin petrol engine. Ohv mechanism in aluminium alloy head; cast-iron cylinder block, dry sump lubrication.
Capacity	624cc (74mm bore x 72.6mm stroke)
Compression ratio	8.7:1
Carburation	Mikuni VM31 (x1)
Max power	50bhp at 6500rpm
Max torque	41lbft at 5500rpm
Ignition system	12V battery and coil
Starting system	Kickstart
Transmission	Four-speed, right-foot shift, return change
Clutch	Multi-disc, wet plate, left-hand clutch lever
Primary reduction	2.26
Gearing	2.54, 1.71, 1.22, 1.00
Final reduction	2.16
Overall drive ratio	4.88
Frame type	Tubular, duplex cradle (double loop)
Suspension	Telescopic fork front, swing-arm rear
Tyre sizes	3.25-18 front, 3.50-18 rear
Brakes (F)	Drum with right hand lever operation
Brakes (R)	Drum with left foot pedal operation
Length	2125mm (83.7in)
Wheelbase	1415mm (55.7in)
Height	1060mm (41.7in)
Width	880mm (34.6in)
Ground clearance	140mm (5.5in)
Weight	181kg (398lb)
Top speed	115mph (185kph)
Standing-quarter	13.8 seconds

650 W1 (domestic version) leading specifications

As per 650 W1 (export version), except:

Max power	47bhp at 6500rpm
Max torque	39lbft at 5500rpm
Primary reduction	2.35
Overall drive ratio	5.10
Length	2135mm (84.1in)
Wheelbase	1420mm (55.9in)
Height	1090mm (42.9in)
Width	865mm (34.0in)
Weight	199kg (438lb)
Top speed	113mph (180kph)

650 W2SS leading specifications

As per 650 W1 (export version), except:

Compression ratio	9.0:1
Carburation	Mikuni VM28 (x2)
Max power	53bhp at 7000rpm
Final reduction	2.33
Overall drive ratio	5.28
Tyre sizes	3.25-19 front, 4.00-18 rear
Length	2115mm (83.3in)
Height	1070mm (42.1in)
Ground clearance	150mm (5.9in)
Standing-quarter	13.7 seconds

650 W1SS leading specifications

As per 650 W1 (export version), except:

Tyre sizes	3.25-19 front, 4.00-18 rear

Length	2115mm (83.3in)
Height	1070mm (42.1in)
Ground clearance	150mm (5.9in)

650 W1S leading specifications

As per W2SS, except:

Primary reduction	2.35
Overall drive ratio	5.47
Length	2145mm (84.4in)
Wheelbase	1420mm (55.9in)
Height	1100mm (43.3in)
Width	865mm (34.0in)
Ground clearance	145mm (5.7in)
Weight	199kg (438lb)

650 W2TT leading specifications

As per W2SS, apart from raised exhaust arrangement.

650 W1SA leading specifications

As per W2SS, except:

Carburation	Mikuni VM28SC (x2)
Transmission	Four-speed, left foot shift, return change
Brakes (R)	Drum with right foot pedal operation
Length	2135mm (84.1in)
Wheelbase	1420mm (55.9in)
Height	1100mm (43.3in)
Width	850mm (33.5in)
Ground clearance	145mm (5.7in)
Weight	199kg (438lb)

650 W3 leading specifications

As per W2SS, except:

Carburation	Mikuni VM28 (x2)
Transmission	Four-speed, left foot shift, return change
Brakes (F)	Dual discs with right hand lever operation
Brakes (R)	Drum with right foot pedal operation
Length	2150mm (84.6in)
Wheelbase	1420mm (55.9in)
Height	1120mm (44.1in)
Width	860mm (33.8in)
Ground clearance	140mm (5.5in)
Weight	215kg (473lb)

Notes: The W1P was the police version of the W1. Likewise the W1SP and W1SAP were police versions of the W1S and W1SA, respectively. Just to confuse matters, there was also a W2P (basically a W1SP), although the W2P was actually released first, with the W1SP following!

PRODUCTION FIGURES

This section shows the calendar year (CY) production figures for each of the original W-series variants, arranged in alphabetical order. For reference and interest, the annual total for all W models is added in the 'All W' column, and the total for all Kawasaki bikes is also listed alongside for each year in the 'All KAC' column. Even though sales continued into the early part of 1976, no W-series models were built beyond December 1974.

Year	W1	W1P	W1S	W1SA	W1SAP	W1SP	W1SS
1965	55	0	0	0	0	0	0
1966	2419	25	0	0	0	0	0
1967	797	192	160	0	0	0	201
1968	8	112	1929	0	0	0	50
1969	0	0	2759	0	0	274	0
1970	0	0	3663	0	0	206	0
1971	0	0	0	4463	121	0	0
1972	0	0	0	1714	86	0	0
1973	0	0	0	0	0	0	0
1974	0	0	0	0	0	0	0
Total	3279	329	8511	6177	207	480	251

Year	W2P	W2SS	W2TT	W3	All W	All KAC
1965	0	0	0	0	55	58,682
1966	0	0	0	0	2444	66,965
1967	12	1221	0	0	2583	72,985
1968	48	729	624	0	3500	79,033
1969	0	41	15	0	3089	107,568
1970	0	5	0	0	3874	140,307
1971	0	0	0	0	4584	192,867
1972	0	0	0	1003	2803	188,149
1973	0	0	0	1728	1728	238,531
1974	0	0	0	1599	1599	311,221
Total	60	1996	639	4330	26,259	-----

APPENDIX II

CLASSIC H-SERIES SPECIFICATIONS & PRODUCTION FIGURES

SPECIFICATIONS

Specifications relate to the original version of each grade, although most continued with the same specs throughout their production life. Any mid-run changes are noted within the text.

500 H1 Mach III (US export version) leading specifications

Engine type	Air-cooled two-stroke vertical-triple petrol engine. Piston-port mechanism in aluminium alloy block with cast-iron liners; alloy head, dry sump lubrication.
Capacity	498cc (60mm bore x 58.8mm stroke)
Compression ratio	6.8:1
Carburation	Mikuni VM28SC (x3)
Max power	60bhp at 7500rpm
Max torque	42lbft at 7000rpm
Ignition system	Capacitive discharge type (CDI)
Starting system	Kickstart
Transmission	Five-speed, left-foot shift, return change
Clutch	Multi-disc, wet plate, left-hand clutch lever
Primary reduction	2.41
Gearing	2.20, 1.40, 1.09, 0.92, 0.81
Final reduction	2.81
Overall drive ratio	5.28
Frame type	Tubular, duplex cradle (double loop)
Suspension	Telescopic fork front, swing-arm rear
Tyre sizes	3.25-19 front, 4.00-18 rear
Brakes (F)	Drum with right hand lever operation
Brakes (R)	Drum with right foot pedal operation
Length	2095mm (82.5in)
Wheelbase	1400mm (55.1in)
Height	1080mm (42.5in)
Width	840mm (33.0in)
Ground clearance	135mm (5.3in)
Weight	174kg (383lb)
Top speed	124mph (198kph)
Standing-quarter	12.4 seconds

500 H1 Mach III (European export version) leading specifications

As per 500 H1 Mach III (US export version), except:

Ignition system	12V battery and three coils

500 H1 Mach III (domestic version) leading specifications

As per 500 H1 Mach III (US export version), except:

Final reduction	3.00
Overall drive ratio	5.84
Top speed	119mph (190kph)

750 H2 Mach IV (all markets) leading specifications

Engine type	Air-cooled two-stroke vertical-triple petrol engine. Piston-port mechanism in aluminium alloy block with cast-iron liners; alloy head, dry sump lubrication.
Capacity	748cc (71mm bore x 63mm stroke)
Compression ratio	7.0:1
Carburation	Mikuni VM30SC (x3)
Max power	74bhp at 6800rpm
Max torque	57lbft at 6500rpm
Ignition system	Capacitive discharge type (CDI)
Starting system	Kickstart
Transmission	Five-speed, left-foot shift, return change
Clutch	Multi-disc, wet plate, left-hand clutch lever

Primary reduction	1.88
Gearing	2.17, 1.47, 1.11, 0.92, 0.81
Final reduction	3.13
Overall drive ratio	4.76
Frame type	Tubular, duplex cradle (double loop)
Suspension	Telescopic fork front, swing-arm rear
Tyre sizes	3.25-19 front, 4.00-18 rear
Brakes (F)	Single disc with right hand lever operation
Brakes (R)	Drum with right foot pedal operation
Length	2080mm (81.9in)
Wheelbase	1410mm (55.5in)
Height	1145mm (45.0in)
Width	850mm (33.5in)
Ground clearance	175mm (6.9in)
Weight	192kg (422lb)
Top speed	126mph (202kph)
Standing-quarter	12.0 seconds

PRODUCTION FIGURES

This section shows the calendar year (CY) production figures for each of the original H-series variants. For reference and interest, the annual total for all H models is added in the 'All H' column, and the total for all Kawasaki bikes is also listed alongside for each year in the 'All KAC' column. The 1975 H1 figures will include a small percentage of KH500-badged models, while the 1976 numbers are all KH500s.

Year	H1	H1-R	H2	H2-R	All H	All KAC
1968	2211	0	0	0	2211	79,033
1969	15,230	70	0	0	15,300	107,568
1970	20,591	15	12	0	20,618	140,307
1971	22,132	30	15,945	0	38,107	192,867
1972	19,521	0	14,016	10	33,547	188,149
1973	15,389	0	7813	3	23,205	238,531
1974	15,764	0	8895	1	24,660	311,221
1975	4903	0	800	0	5703	207,038
1976	1768	0	0	0	1768	201,721
Total	117,509	115	47,481	14	165,119	-----

APPENDIX III

EARLY Z-SERIES SPECIFICATIONS & PRODUCTION FIGURES

SPECIFICATIONS

Specifications relate to the original version of each grade, although most continued with the the same specs throughout their production life. Any mid-run changes are noted within the text.

Z1 (US version) leading specifications

Engine type	Air-cooled four-stroke inline-four petrol engine. Dohc mechanism in aluminium alloy head; aluminium alloy casing, wet sump lubrication.
Capacity	903cc (66mm bore x 66mm stroke)
Compression ratio	8.5:1
Carburation	Mikuni VM28SC (x4)
Max power	82bhp at 8500rpm
Max torque	54lbft at 7000rpm
Ignition system	12V battery and coil
Starting system	Electric with kickstart back-up
Transmission	Five-speed, left-foot shift, return change
Clutch	Multi-disc, wet plate, left-hand clutch lever
Primary reduction	1.73
Gearing	3.17, 2.19, 1.67, 1.38, 1.22
Final reduction	2.33
Overall drive ratio	4.92
Frame type	Tubular, duplex cradle (double loop)
Suspension	Telescopic fork front, swing-arm rear
Tyre sizes	3.25-19 front, 4.00-18 rear
Brakes (F)	Single disc with right hand lever operation
Brakes (R)	Drum with right foot pedal operation
Length	2205mm (86.8in)
Wheelbase	1490mm (58.7in)
Height	1150mm (45.3in)
Width	800mm (31.5in)
Ground clearance	160mm (6.3in)
Weight	230kg (506lb)
Top speed	128mph (205kph)
Standing-quarter	12.0 seconds

Z1 (European version) leading specifications

As per Z1 (US version), except:

Length	2250mm (88.6in)
Height	1175mm (46.3in)
Width	820mm (32.3in)

Z2 leading specifications

As per Z1 (US version), except:

Capacity	746cc (64mm bore x 58mm stroke)
Compression ratio	9.0:1
Carburation	Mikuni VM26SC (x4)
Max power	69bhp at 9000rpm
Max torque	43lbft at 7500rpm
Final reduction	2.80
Overall drive ratio	5.90
Length	2200mm (86.6in)
Wheelbase	1500mm (59.0in)
Height	1170mm (46.1in)
Width	865mm (34.1in)
Ground clearance	165mm (6.5in)
Weight	232kg (510lb)
Top speed	118mph (189kph)
Standing-quarter	12.5 seconds

PRODUCTION FIGURES

This section shows the calendar year (CY) production figures for each of the early Z-series variants. For reference and interest, the annual total for all early Z models is added in the 'All Z' column, and the total for all Kawasaki bikes is also listed alongside for each year in the 'All KAC' column. The figures for 1975 will include a percentage of 1976 MY KZ900- and K900-badged models. There may also be a handful of extra Z2s built in January 1976, which is when the Z750F officially took its place on the line.

Year	Z1	Z1P	Z2	Z2P	All Z	All KAC
1972	10,896	4	516	4	11,420	188,149
1973	29,841	0	4292	30	34,163	238,531
1974	36,842	320	5808	0	42,970	311,221
1975	27,510	200	6374	0	34,084	207,038
Total	105,089	524	16,990	34	122,637	-----

Note: The Lincoln-built machines, although manufactured from August 1975, were 1976 MY bikes, and are therefore not classed as the main subject matter for this book. For the record, a total of 15,148 KZ900A and KZ900B models were built in America during 1975.

Written in a friendly and engaging manner by an experienced enthusiast, this manual provides a thorough and detailed restoration guide complete with hundreds of original colour photos. This is the author's third restoration guide, his previous works having been well-received by both professional and amateur restorers alike.

ISBN: 978-1-787111-58-5

Paperback • 27x20.7cm • 224 pages • 794 pictures

For more information and price details, visit our website at www.veloce.co.uk • email: info@veloce.co.uk • Tel: +44(0)1305 260068

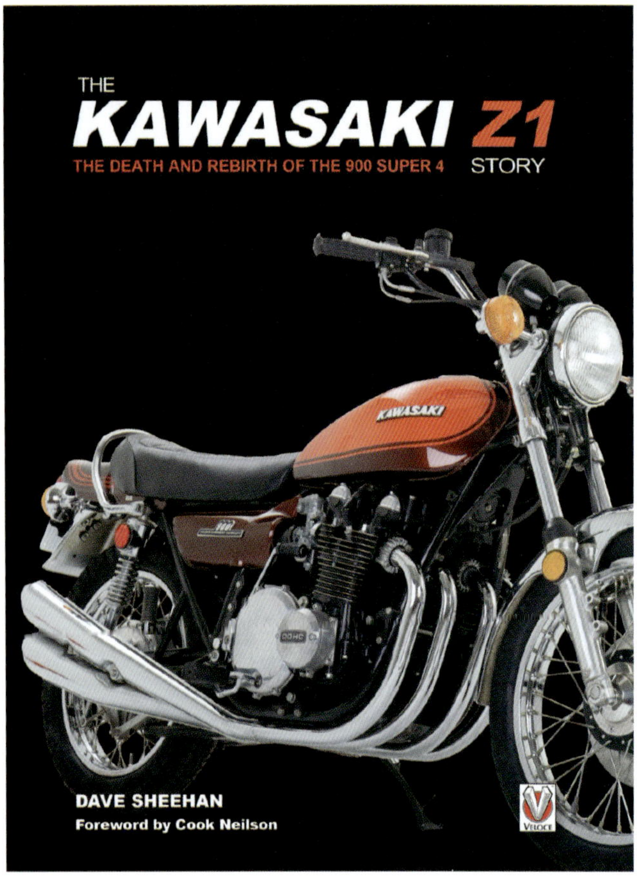

The Kawasaki Z1 Story tells how the smallest of Japan's Big Four motorcycle manufacturers nearly beat the world's biggest to become the first to the market with a Four, and how Honda's CB750 debut almost spelled the end for the Z-1 … before Kawasaki stunned everybody with something bigger, faster, and better!

ISBN: 978-1-845848-07-1
Paperback • 21x14.8cm • 256 pages • 135 pictures

Having this book in your pocket is just like having a real marque expert at your side. Benefit from David Orritt's years of ownership, learn how to spot a bad bike quickly and how to assess a promising bike like a professional. Get the right bike at the right price!

ISBN: 978-1-845845-23-0
Paperback • 19.5x13.9cm • 64 pages
• 93 colour pictures

For more information and price details, visit our website at www.veloce.co.uk • email: info@veloce.co.uk
• Tel: +44(0)1305 260068

INDEX

The Kawasaki (KHI) company's subsidiaries and products are mentioned throughout this book.